Just Call Me Rae

Ann Weimer Moxley

Just Call Me Rae

The Story of Rae O. Weimer, Founder of the University of Florida College of Journalism and Communications

University of Florida College of Journalism and Communications · *Gainesville*

Published in the United States of America

29 28 27 26 25 24 6 5 4 3 2 1

Library of Congress Cataloging-in-Publication Data
Names: Moxley, Ann Weimer, 1946– author.
Title: Just call me Rae : the story of Rae O. Weimer, founder of the University of Florida College of Journalism and Communications / Ann Weimer Moxley.
Other titles: Story of Rae O. Weimer, founder of the University of Florida College of Journalism and Communications
Description: 1st. | Gainesville : University of Florida College of Journalism and Communications, [2023] | Includes bibliographical references and index. | Summary: "Just Call Me Rae chronicles the life of the man who pioneered journalism education in Florida and built one of the most innovative journalism and communications programs in the country"—Provided by publisher.
Identifiers: LCCN 2023046423 (print) | LCCN 2023046424 (ebook) | ISBN 9798987960509 (hardback) | ISBN 9798987960516 (ebook)
Subjects: LCSH: Weimer, Rae O. | University of Florida. College of Journalism and Communications—History—Biography. | Journalism—Study and teaching—Florida—Gainesville—Biography. | BISAC: BIOGRAPHY & AUTOBIOGRAPHY / Editors, Journalists, Publishers | BIOGRAPHY & AUTOBIOGRAPHY / Educators
Classification: LCC LD1792.65.W35 M68 2023 (print) | LCC LD1792.65.W35 (ebook) | DDC 378.1/11092 [B]—dc23/eng/20231027
LC record available at https://lccn.loc.gov/2023046423
LC ebook record available at https://lccn.loc.gov/2023046424

Produced by the University Press of Florida

Published by the University of Florida College
of Journalism and Communications
1885 Stadium Road
Gainesville, FL 32611

To all the journalists who provide unbiased, critical information and advocate for truth, fairness, and equality.

Contents

Preface

The inspiration for this book came first from a close high school friend, Dr. Bruce Stechmiller, who had known my father. Bruce felt my father's remarkable story of creating first the School, and later the College, of Journalism and Communications at the University of Florida, as well as my father's work for the remarkable newspaper experiment that was *PM*, should be told. Bruce encouraged me to write my father's story.

I knew that some years before his death, my father had dictated his life story on cassette tapes, which were then transcribed by his wife and my stepmother, Wilma. However, I had never bothered to read the manuscripts and wasn't sure what had happened to them or the cassette tapes. After Bruce's challenge, I located over 400 pages typed by Wilma. As I read through the manuscript, I was fascinated with my father's early life. These pages gave me the basis to edit his memoirs and bring them to the printed page.

As my dad told about historical events he directly experienced, I began to do my own research into these episodes, learning much about the early twentieth century. He related incidents and experiences in his life of which I had no prior knowledge. Other materials in my possession included some of the actual copies of *PM* from the 1940s as well as documents from the staff; photos and publications from the University of Florida's College of Journalism and Communications; letters to and regarding my father from his friends and admirers, all of which have been incorporated into this biographical memoir. I truly regret not having read the transcribed pages while my father was still alive to glean even more historical information as well as more about his perspective. So, telling his story now is my tribute to a remarkable man.

A number of individuals were particularly helpful in bringing this project to fruition. First, I want to thank my husband, Jim Solar, for his support, suggestions, and editing of my work. Margaret Gaylord, senior director of advancement and alumni relations for the College of Journalism and Communications, was instrumental in bringing the parties together to publish this work. Next, the advice and publishing information I received from Romi Gutierrez, director of the University Press of Florida, was invaluable. Finally, I appreciate Randy Bennett, executive director for external relations at the University of Florida's College of Journalism and Communications, for his assistance in obtaining some of the photographs of my father to include in this book. A special thank you is due to Hub Brown, dean of the College of Journalism and Communications, for enabling this project to be completed.

Ann Weimer Moxley

Introduction

Can a man without a college degree become a university dean? Well, it happened at the University of Florida and this is the real story.

Beginning in 1903, Rae Weimer's story provides a unique picture of Midwest rural life at the beginning of the twentieth century. As Rae related, growing up in a small farming community in Nebraska in his early years instilled in him a sense of adventure and required resourcefulness. The Weimer family's small farm did not provide sufficient income for a family of four, so Rae and his family devised a fascinating assortment of means to earn a living. These endeavors afforded him a variety of experiences and enabled him to gain an understanding and appreciation for the laborer, the farmer, and the common man. Some of his jobs included trapping animals, breaking horses, laying track for the railroad, and delivering newspapers. He tells of many other ingenious and innovative ways to make ends meet as he paints a picture of what life was like in a small Midwestern town during this historical time.

Although Rae was working his way through college, he was forced to leave after three years because of a lack of funds. As a rambling journalist moving from paper to paper throughout the Midwest during the depression era, Rae spent the next quarter century learning by working in the newspaper business. In this book you will see how he lived and coped through his eyes.

Rae's longest newspaper stint was the eight years he worked as the managing editor for one of the boldest experiments in journalism—a daily newspaper that hired the best writers, photographers, and journalists but did not sell any advertising. A newspaper whose motto was, "We don't like people who push other people around." Much has been written over the years about Ralph Ingersoll's experimental, but short-lived, New York daily newspaper, *PM*—more than can, or should, be included in this biography. You will learn the *PM* story from Rae's perspective and why it was important in his life. After *PM* suspended publication, Rae's experience and reputation at the paper undoubtedly led to his hiring by the University of Florida in their small journalism department.

Even in the face of challenges and adversity, Rae, ever the optimist, never let his problems get him down. He had learned the lessons of hard work, resourcefulness, and innovation to cope from his parents. He took life as it came. Unforeseen circumstances altered Rae's dreams, reshaping his career path. When obstacles arose, Rae, undiscouraged, found other avenues to pursue.

What made this peripatetic journalist finally settle in one place? Was it that he found a fit with his life philosophy to help his fellow man? Was it meeting another like-minded newspaper woman who wanted to share his life and raise a family rather than focusing just on her own career? In Ruth Meister, Rae Weimer found a partner whose first priority was her family, yet she still found it possible to use her own journalistic talents and serve her community while supporting her husband's career.

An anecdote Rae told about himself encapsulates his personality. When he first arrived at the University of Florida, without a college degree, a professor asked Rae how he would like to be addressed—Dean Weimer, Dr. Weimer, Professor Weimer? Rae replied, "You can just call me Rae." Long after Rae retired in 1974, he finally became a "man of letters" when the university awarded him an honorary doctor of letters. Rae was instrumental in the evolution of the small department of journalism into the School of Journalism and Communications and finally, into one of the nation's most highly acclaimed Colleges of Journalism and Communications, making Rae a dean without a college degree, the culmination of his incredible career in journalism. Beyond that, he was highly respected by the university's academia, a civic leader in his community, and a mentor to generations of young journalists.

How did this man of limited means and no college degree found one of the country's most prestigious journalism institutions? What were the forces that shaped who he would become? Was it his early exposure to the everyday common folk—the farmer, the laborer, the union member—that fashioned his moral principles? Rae Weimer was a true humanist who cared about fairness and equality. Certainly, his older brother had a tremendous impact on the path Rae's life would follow.

The brothers often worked together for many of the same organizations. Another influence was working for the Scripps-Howard newspaper chain, known for its support of unions and the common man, and then for *PM* with its very liberal philosophy.

Most of Rae's story is told in his own words recorded in 1988. Had Rae not set out to tell his own life story, we would not know what factors molded his personality and set him on the path to success. We would not know how he faced adversity and overcame obstacles. There is no other information about his early life and the influences that eventually led him to the University of Florida, save a few quotes from interviews and transcriptions of the cassette tapes he recorded eight years before his death. Without the background story told by Rae himself, we could not answer these questions. Most of those who knew Rae best are now deceased, leaving little documentation or memories of his life. Much more is known of Rae's later years at the University of Florida because of items written by colleagues and journalists. What follows is the life story of this scion of pioneers who himself was a pioneer in Florida journalism.

PART I

Native Nebraskan

1 Scion of Pioneers

America as we know it today was largely founded by immigrants, Rae Weimer's family among them. "The Weimer Saga dates back to Germany and probably to Weimar, Germany, at least on the paternal side," Rae believed. "My mother's ancestors, Fosters and Wilders, came from Great Britain. One of the voids in my family history is a record dating back to the immigration to America. The data I document comes from the family Bible, which recorded births, marriages, and deaths in pioneer times. For decades such records from family Bibles were accepted in the legal system because no such evidence was kept by the local governments for births, deaths, and marriages. Even up into the twentieth century there were no local records kept by the counties of births in Nebraska."

Internet searches yield ancestral records for Rae's family dating back to the late 1500s in Europe. Although "Weimer" in German translates as "one who came from Weimar," the first mention of the Weimer name in genealogy was Michel Weimer, born in 1624 in the Lower Rhine region of Alsace, France. Many of Rae's paternal ancestors hailed from all over Germany as well as a few from England and a number from Alsace. The majority of these ancestors immigrated to Pennsylvania and then joined other early settlers moving westward, first to Ohio and Illinois, and then on to Nebraska. The maternal Foster side of his family had roots in Great Britain—England, Scotland, and Ireland—and possibly in America among Native Americans. Ancestral records that abound today on the internet were not available during his life, so Rae did not know of his rich ancestral history, but he did know the path his forefathers paved: "Both sets of my grandparents were pioneers. As newlyweds, each couple joined in that ever increasing movement of the mid-1800s to push the frontier ever westward." As more of the wilderness was settled for farming, more people continued moving west.

Although he had no recollection of his mother's parents, Rae did know of their history: "My mother's parents, Franklin H. Foster and Mary Elizabeth Wilder, were married in 1878 at Beaver Crossing, Nebraska. Shortly after they were married they moved to Seward, Nebraska, where Franklin established his office as a land agent. Two daughters, Kittie Mable Foster, my mother, and Emma Clara Foster, were born in Seward on November 28, 1879, and September 28, 1881, respectively. Intrigued by the federal government's distribution of vast acres of land, Franklin Foster packed up his family, boarded a train and arrived in Mason City, Nebraska, about 1885—the farthest west the Burlington Railroad operated at that time. The arrival of the railroad had been a great incentive for settlement and expansion of the state. It was not a long-lasting happy move. Emma died at the age of twelve in 1893, her death at such an early age [apparently from] some common childhood disease and lack of medical care. [My maternal grandfather] died five years later and my maternal grandmother died in 1906, meaning neither she nor her husband reached the age of fifty. My mother did have a grandmother, Jane Wilder, who lived in Pomona, California, but I never met my great grandmother."

In contrast to not knowing his maternal grandparents, Rae noted, "The only relatives I ever came to know well were those on the Weimer side of the family. Until I left for college, I had frequent contacts with my paternal grandparents, but did not have the foresight to question them about family history. What a loss! Even if they had no records, the stories they could have told would have been of great value to their descendants." Partly for this reason, Rae dictated his own story and life history.

Rae's auburn-haired paternal grandfather, David F. Weimer, was born in Harrison County, Ohio, in 1839. "I was very fond of my [paternal] grandfather, David F. Weimer," Rae remembered, "and had many contacts with him in my early childhood." During the Civil War, David enlisted in the 19th Ohio Volunteer Infantry of the Union Army at age twenty-one. David, perhaps the first "journalist" in the family, kept a diary consisting of three or four small pocket notebooks chronicling his Civil War experiences. Although never wounded, he suffered many privations, including almost starving to death, as a prisoner of war for fourteen months. First captured in the Battle of Stones River, or Murfreesboro, in

January 1863, he was transported by train, then marched from place to place until the prisoners, some clad only in threadbare blankets, arrived at Camp Parole, Maryland, where they found smallpox, mumps, cold, and hunger. On the night of February 15, David Weimer and four others "broke for home." For twelve days, the escapees dodged picket lines, forded icy streams, begged for scraps of food, and slept in sheds and ditches until they crossed the Pennsylvania state line and found haven at Morrisons Cove. David then returned to his unit and served his country until he was again captured at the Battle of Chickamauga in September 1863 by the "sesech," as he called the Confederates, and transferred first to Belle Island and then Libby Prison, both near Richmond, Virginia. He eventually ended up in the most infamous of Civil War prisons, Camp Sumter, or Andersonville as it was more commonly known. David estimated there were some 30,000 soldiers in a large, fifteen-acre stockade with only minimal shelter, clothing, food, or water. His imprisonment left David in poor health from which he never really recovered. David was able to return home to Ohio in 1865 to marry his sweetheart, Mary Kryder. Both were natives of Ohio. "As I understand, the Weimer family was the first family to get a federal land grant in the state of Ohio," Rae recalled. "There were a lot of Weimers in Ohio and until the late 1920s there was a large Weimer reunion held there each year with several hundred people present."

Seven years after their marriage, David and Mary Weimer were among the earliest settlers in Nebraska as Rae tells. "My paternal grandparents, too, joined pioneers moving westward, first to Illinois where three daughters were born. When the Nebraska Territory became the thirty-seventh state in the Union in 1867, word soon spread of vast farmlands being opened up for settlers in the new state. It was too much for pioneering families to resist. My paternal grandparents, David and Mary Weimer, packed up their belongings and three small children, crossed the Mississippi River, came across Iowa and crossed the Missouri River to settle in Otoe County in southeastern Nebraska." There, a fourth daughter and a son were born followed by Rae's father, Curtis, on October 26, 1876, the youngest of five siblings.

The Weimers later settled in the Ortello Valley, where Rae's paternal grandfather, David Weimer, established a Sunday school in his sod house. One of Rae's aunts and her family also lived in a sod house on a farm eight miles from town. Settlers of the Great Plains found sod a free, as well as plentiful, alternative for housing construction when timber or stone was scarce. Sod homes had the advantage of being fireproof in areas prone to grass fires. They provided excellent insulation—warmer in the winter and cooler in the summer than homes constructed from other materials. Unlike common lawn grass today, the sod house was constructed from a number of prairie grasses with densely packed roots, which held the soil together. The sod was then cut into "bricks" and stacked to form two-foot-thick walls. Scarce wood was used only for framing doors and windows. This method of building homes was common in the second half of the nineteenth century until the railroad made more modern building materials readily accessible.

An intelligent and determined woman, Kittie Foster was the backbone of the Weimer family. Rae admired many of his mother's qualities. He tells of one challenge she overcame in her youth: "In early childhood my mother was left-handed. She learned to write and work with her left hand, which her parents accepted as natural. But early in elementary school, a male teacher informed her that he did not permit students in his class to write with the left hand. Whether she alternated hands in other classes I don't know, but throughout her adult life she wrote very well with either hand without any marked difference. My mother . . . was the first girl to graduate from the high school. She and two boys comprised the first high school graduating class in Mason City, Nebraska."

When Rae's paternal grandmother, Mary, died at age 101 in 1925, the local newspaper hailed her as one of the "real pioneer mothers of Nebraska and Custer County." Grandma Weimer always looked on the bright side of life and accepted the privations and toil of pioneer life with fortitude, traits she may have passed on to her grandson, Rae Weimer, who became a journalism pioneer. In addition to Grandma Weimer's optimism, willingness to work hard, and perseverance, Rae later displayed other characteristics of the early pioneers including honesty, humility, close ties to family, and an eagerness to help others in the community.

2 On the Frontier

Settlers in the nineteenth century were more isolated than those living in the eastern part of the United States. "It is apparent that people did not travel in very wide circles in those pioneer days," Rae explained. "My Grandfather and Grandmother Weimer were born within thirty-five miles of each other in Ohio, and my mother's parents came from Beaver Crossing, Nebraska, not far from where both my mother and father were born. The two families moved to Custer County within a few years of each other but did not meet until they each moved to Mason City, Nebraska, a small community of a few hundred residents in the very center of Nebraska. When it was officially incorporated as a municipality in 1886, it was the western terminus of the Burlington Railroad. Mason City was not only the western terminus of the railroad at that time, but also the first municipality in Custer County to be served by the railroad. Even with towns springing up east and west of Mason City, the town remained the center of a large farming area with no cities or towns within forty to fifty miles to the north or south. It was still a very small community of about 500 residents when I graduated from high school in 1922." The most likely origin of the name, Mason, as the railroad always called it, was in honor of Oliver Perry Mason, a former Nebraska Supreme Court Judge.

Cattle ranchers from Texas were the first white men to settle in Custer County in the latter part of the nineteenth century. By 1880 there were 60,000 head of cattle on Custer County's open range. Around this time, a homesteader migration began to supplant the cattlemen to their chagrin. These permanent pioneers made the value of Custer County's agricultural production greater than any other Nebraska county even today.[1]

Rae recalled his family's pioneer roots, "Dreams of vast acres of fertile farmland obviously drew my ancestors and thousands of other pioneers westward into Nebraska. After brief stops, my forefathers pushed on westward and eventually settled in the very center of the state in Custer County. Nebraska—the wide open spaces where the west began—is an Indian name meaning 'flat water' derived from the Platte River [which] flows almost the full length of the state and in some places is more than a half mile wide." The Platte River played an important role in the westward expansion because portions of many trails taken by early settlers followed this "mile wide and inch deep" muddy river including the Oregon, California, and Mormon trails, plus the Pony Express route.

The nickname "Cornhusker State" derives from the millions of bushels of corn that were grown here. Rae recounted other aspects of Nebraska's agricultural history: "The state offered diversified opportunities in agriculture with thousands of acres in the western Sand Hills for large herds of beef cattle grazing on prairie grass, wheat fields south of the Platte River as far as the eye could see, and more than 100,000 farms and ranches in between. The state bragged it had more farms per capita than any other state in the union. As metropolitan areas developed, the number of farms and ranches was reduced to around 60,000. Omaha, the state's largest city, was once the world's largest beef market." By 1955, Omaha had overtaken Chicago to become the world's largest livestock market.[2]

At the beginning of the twentieth century, over half America's population lived on small, diversified farms in rural areas rather than the large corporate-owned farms of today.[3] Families went from being self-sufficient in growing and producing their own food to raising crops and animals for profit to supplement their income and augment their standard of living. The horse was indispensable to the farmer who used this animal to till his fields and as a means of transportation in the absence of automobiles. Rae's family had a horse and buggy with rubber tires for transportation. Life could be challenging in the absence of modern conveniences such as electricity, indoor plumbing, air-conditioning, central heating, and even paved streets in these small rural communities.

Rae experienced just such a life in the farming community of Mason City as he described: "Not only was Mason City in the center of Nebraska but it was in the center of the great agricultural section of America in the early twentieth century. Much of the commercial enterprise in town was focused on agriculture and geared to serve a wider population than just those who lived in town. Peak shopping day was Saturday. Unless it was harvest season or the time of year for 'putting up hay' or 'laying by' corn, all the farmers and their families funneled into town on Saturday. Many stayed until after the Saturday night movie. Women from the farms brought a variety of products to sell to the local stores including butter, eggs, chickens, ducks, and vegetables. In the afternoon men and women visited on benches in front of the stores or stood in small clusters to catch up on the latest happenings in the community. Children would hie off to the matinee, and some men could always be found by the livery stable pitching horseshoes. The blacksmith shop did more business for the rural population than for the townsfolk, primarily repairing farm machinery and furnishing replacement parts. In the fall, when the ground became frozen and slippery, the blacksmith would attach steel shoes to the horses.

"In my earliest recollections of Mason City, there was a butcher shop, a drugstore, a hardware store, a bank, and four general stores. Each general store carried groceries; one specialized in clothing, another in shoes, and a third in furniture but also served as the undertaker. The town had no electricity, sewers, or paving. There were two barber shops, one Saturday-only movie house, two variety stores, a telephone exchange, and a small city hall where the town council met and where church women served chicken dinners on Election Day as a fundraiser. Mason had four churches. The largest was the First Baptist where my family worshipped. The other denominations were Methodist, Christian, and Catholic. There were two grain elevators adjacent to the railroad, a cement block–making plant, a doctor's office, two blacksmith shops, and a livery stable. At the height of growth, which was never very great, there was a creamery established on the 'other side' of the railroad tracks. Adjacent to the depot were the stockyards for assembling hogs and cattle for shipping to the Omaha market. As I mentioned, for many years the town had one movie house. I can recall attending Saturday matinees before I was old enough to go to school. Admission was five or ten cents to see such thrilling cinema as *The Perils of Pauline* or comedians such as Harold Lloyd and Fatty Arbuckle.

"Because Mason City never had any paved streets in my youth, rainstorms could leave the streets in front of stores in quite a quagmire. My early recollection of that area was of ten-foot-wide boardwalks in front of the stores. When the planks were later removed to install concrete walks, youngsters followed along the ripping-up process to look for coins that might have dropped between the planks.

"My father and mother were married in Mason City on October 30, 1901. My brother, Claude (later known as Doc), was born June 18, 1902, and I followed eighteen months [*sic*] later on November 2, 1903. Both of us were born at home in a small-frame, two-bedroom house because there was no hospital in Mason City, nor, probably, in the entire county at that time. It was a common occurrence for births to take place in homes.

"I have no recollection of that home—the only house I recall in Mason was about a block from my parents' original home. I suspect the two additions to the family in short order prompted my parents to consider a larger house. But they probably overdid it. About a block south of where we originally lived, my parents built a three-story house, doubtless the tallest house in town at the time. [The house was built on an inclined lot, which continued for some 200 yards beyond the house to the top of a hill where an underground cistern was built along with a 160-foot well and windmill, giving the house its own water system.] That much altitude gave pressure sufficient to [provide] water in the house, including for our hot water furnace and radiators on the first and second floors. Cistern water was piped into the kitchen and in the bathroom for a lavatory and bathtub. There was no indoor toilet initially. Later, we took the partition out between the bathroom and bedroom and made it into a bath with complete indoor plumbing."

The house had a large porch on two sides. A full basement encompassed a room for canned fruit, another for several tons of coal and the furnace, a laundry room, and a room for Rae's mother to operate five chicken incubators in the winter with an additional space for Doc's experimental electric shop. Above the second floor, with its five bedrooms, was an unfinished third floor with no heating or plumbing of any kind, and above that was an attic for storage and play on rainy days. To Rae, it was always a mystery why his parents built a home with so much space for a family of four, or how it was financed. He speculated that his father may have anticipated having a larger family.

Rae and his older brother were very close throughout their lives, working together on the farm, in the newspaper business, and finally residing in Florida: Rae in Gainesville and Doc in St. Petersburg. In fact, Doc was Rae's best friend in childhood. Parents often based their children's names on other family members as Rae explained although he never revealed the origin of his first name: "Interestingly, my brother and I received our middle names from grandparents. My mother's father was Franklin Hayes Foster and my brother's middle name was Franklin. The parents of my maternal grandmother were Otis and Jane Wilder so I received my middle name, Otis. But in childhood, I was known as 'Bill Weimer' until I went away to college and then I acquired the nickname my father feared I would have and tried to avoid of 'Red' Weimer in reference to my auburn hair. Later in life my father called me 'Bill Dugan,' I believe after some humorist who either was on a Chautauqua circuit[4] or writing a column. He often referred to me after that as just 'Dugan.' I even used the name Bill Dugan when I [later] wrote a sports column for the [*Olean Herald*]." As a boy, Doc drove for a family doctor in Nebraska, which is how he acquired his nickname. In letters to his brother, Doc would address Rae as "Bill" just as his parents had done.

3 Earning a Livelihood

The Weimers lived in a small Nebraska town of about 500, but they acquired 480 acres three miles south of their home identified as "Weimer's addition" to Mason City on the town plan. "We farmed part of it, leased out part, and ran cattle on a large pasture area," Rae explained.[5] "Our land included an orchard [of apples, cherries, mulberries, plums], which was about a block square, two vegetable gardens [for potatoes, sweet corn, radishes, lettuce, asparagus], a large pasture for our one horse and one or two cows . . . , a fairly large corral, which we used later for cattle [and hogs] in the fall and winter." Dairy cattle provided food for the Weimers, but the beef cattle and hogs would be sold in Omaha when they had a full carload or to a local dealer who collected from other farms and would do the shipping. Earning a sufficient livelihood was always a concern throughout Rae's youth and early adulthood. He acknowledged that "most people had a better income than we did." It is unclear how the Weimers afforded their plots of land, but at the end of the nineteenth century, a severe drought resulted in livestock sold for practically nothing and farms almost given away, as hundreds of settlers evacuated. Rae also believed his paternal grandfather became a fairly prosperous farmer because when the county went broke in the depression of the 1880s, David Weimer was elected treasurer for the county and spent much of his own money to bail out the county.

To support his family, Rae's father, Curtis, had a variety of jobs and other ways of earning money in addition to the farm income. In Rae's youth, Curtis was a paper hanger as well as a painter. "He was a likable guy, extremely outgoing and gregarious," Rae told an interviewer.[6] Portions of the farm were rented out with the Weimers obtaining a share of the crops raised. Later, Curtis left Mason City for a few years when he owned and operated a chain of movie houses around Gothenburg in the Platte River Valley and in Minnesota. Along about the third or fourth grade, Rae remembered him returning home to resume his previous occupations of painting and paper hanging. For a time, Curtis did much of the driving for a local banker using an Abbot touring car owned by the bank. Because Curtis serviced, maintained, and housed this car in his garage, the Weimer family was afforded some limited access to automobile travel.

While still in grade school, Rae and Doc became active in working the farm. The brothers enjoyed the freedoms of country life but accepted the responsibilities that came with farm life. Both morning and night, when not in school, they milked cows, helped raise the chickens, gardened in the summer, picked fruit, and tended the orchard. "We had to shell corn for the chickens and put down hay for the cows—there are a hundred and one things to do when you have livestock!" Rae remembered. "I think it was good training that we had our work laid out for us every day."

"Before electricity came to Mason City, everyone used kerosene lamps," said Rae. "For many years prior to that, we had an acetylene gas lighting system. I think there were three houses in town that had this same unusual contraption." Carbide lamps, or acetylene gas lamps, are simple lamps that produce and burn acetylene created by the reaction of calcium carbide with water. Acetylene gas lamps were used to illuminate buildings, such as lighthouse beacons, and as headlights on motor cars and bicycles. When the carbide was gone, a thick, white, liquid residue had to be disposed of as Rae explained: "This was one of the chores my brother and I had. Initially we would dump paint buckets filled with this residue in the street, making a mess. Then we found out the liquid was a good whitewash for the chicken house to eliminate mites."

Rae began earning money at a young age. "From almost the time I was able to sit on a horse, and that was mighty early in life, my brother and I would ride this horse or hitch it up to a buggy if my mother needed to go to the farm or pick up feed. In those days when I was still very small, I jumped at the opportunity to earn money, and with our one horse . . . I would help my grandfather and another Civil War veteran cultivate their garden. I would ride the horse and pull his cultivator; he would walk alongside and guide the cultivator. Sometimes I would get seventy-five cents or a dollar for a job that might take a half day."

Another source of income, in addition to the share of crops from renters, was selling the evening cows' milk delivered in little quart metal buckets with a lid. Rae's mother sold eggs and chickens, too. The Weimers were the first family in that part of Nebraska to practice caponizing chickens. Caponizing chickens is a delicate surgical operation to remove the testicles and neuter the chicken so the bird can grow larger. The Weimers often sold the capons for Thanksgiving dinner because no turkeys were raised in the area and people generally had chicken for festive occasions. "People were wild to get these capons," Rae said. "They grew much larger than a normal chicken and the meat was [especially] tender, so we had no trouble selling them." The incubators used in the winter were heated by kerosene lamps to keep the temperature at 103 degrees but had to be cleaned daily, another of Rae's chores. The baby chicks would be sold when they hatched at around three weeks. To keep her chickens healthy, Rae's mother would spread straw on the dirt floor, then throw grain on top to make the chickens scratch hard to get the feed, giving them exercise in the winter.

Part of Rae's farm chores included butchering hogs or cattle for the meat and the hides. Leftover scraps were ground up and made into a German dish called *paunhaus.* His mother would put a mixture of ground scraps, half pork and half beef, plus cornmeal and water into a cast-iron kettle next to the fire of wood or corn cobs. She stored the mixture in crocks in the pantry. When cold and solid it could be fried for breakfast. "That was some of the finest eating you can imagine!" Rae reminisced. "Nobody else in Mason knew how to make it and probably didn't want to learn because not very many people in town butchered, but all my mother's friends were anxious that she would give them a little crock of *paunhaus* every year. I discovered another 'so-called' delicacy when I joined a roundup at which young male calves were being castrated. The ranchers would take the testicles, known then as 'mountain oysters,' roll them in flour, and deep fry them. Although everyone thought they were a delicacy, I wished I had brought my own dinner bucket along because I didn't eat much."

Along with other youths, Rae told of another source of income: "One of the moneymaking projects for small fry was picking up copper wire, the bottoms of laundry boilers, and bottles. In those days every family did their own laundry in a boiler. Eventually they burned out and would be discarded. All the kids in town had their eye out for these discarded boilers which was one of the biggest pieces of copper we could find to sell."

In elementary school, Rae and Doc would trap skunks, or sometimes civet cats. "We would go out every day to check the traps," Rae said. "If we [caught one], we would skin it right there and throw the carcass down the draw where coyotes or birds would pick it apart. It is interesting how you prepare the hide: once you split up the hind legs, you pull the bone out of the tail, then cut the skin off by turning it wrong side out working forward. The real technique is to get the skin off with as little fat on it as possible, being careful not to puncture the hide, which diminishes its value. Next, we would stretch the hide over a board, wrong side out, hang it up in the sun to dry, then sell the pelts to the butcher at anywhere from $5 to $10 per pelt. The less white from the stripes, the more valuable the pelt. Civet cats were handled the same way, but they are smaller and rather than a continuous white stripe, there are little dashes of white; of course they were worth much less money than a skunk."

Besides trapping, Rae and a friend also hunted prairie chickens, rabbits, or quail. Rae said, "Our first gun was a .22-caliber rifle ordered from Sears, Roebuck. However, our mother didn't know about it and when she found out, she was a little put out but didn't make us send it back." Later, Rae and his friend hunted with 12-gauge shotguns as Rae recalled. "Jackrabbits were great fun to shoot, probably more than any other thing unless it was a bird on the wing. Rabbits were plentiful and we might get two or three each to bring home. When you shot one, the best thing to do was bleed it right then. You took hold of the rabbit's head, swung it around in a circle to wring its neck, which came off very easily and prevented blood from coagulating in the meat. When we got home we would skin them and our mothers would cook them. One day when we were hunting prairie chickens, a bird flew up and we both fired, hitting what turned out to be a pheasant. It was against the law in those days to shoot pheasants. Since we didn't know quite what to do with it and knew it wouldn't do any good to just let it lay there, we brought it home and ate this delicious treat.

"The opportunity to join a cattle drive arose when I was in high school. One summer there was a severe drought, not unusual in Nebraska, and our pastures dried up. So, all the farmers who were raising cattle got together to drive their cattle up to the Sand Hills where there was pasture. I had never heard of a cattle drive before. This drive lasted three days with two nights on the road. I remember very vividly that we would stop the day's drive outside a town where we could find open space and some grass to bed the cattle down. Sometimes we had to buy a load of hay to feed them. In the fall, ranchers went back to the Sand Hills to drive the cattle back to Mason. Later, when I became a great fan of Louis Lamour books, I knew all about cattle drives out west." Rae never missed an opportunity to earn money or indulge in a new adventure.

In the early 1900s, six independent horse and mule markets in Grand Island, Nebraska, helped supply horses and mules for the French and British armies in World War I; by 1924, the Grand Island Horse and Mule Market was the world's largest, with the last market closing in the 2000s.[7] Buying and reselling western horses was also another Weimer enterprise. But Rae's life would be forever changed by that particular monetary pursuit as he explained, "We would hear that somebody had western horses for sale. We bought them and brought the horses to Mason, keeping them until we had a fair herd before taking them to Grand Island to sell to the Army at the largest horse market in the world. Mostly on weekends when we weren't in school, we might catch one of these horses, put a saddle and bridle on it, and then break it to ride. We'd get a little more money, maybe $10 or $15, if we could show it was broken to ride." Rae told Ron Sercombe, "I used to get a charge out of going to the corral with my buddies after the cowboys had rounded up some wild horses. I broke and gentled many wild horses. Maybe I got overconfident.[8]

"One late summer or early fall day when I was about fifteen, a real bucker threw me. I hit the dirt on my right arm, fractured my wrist and knocked what is known as the 'crazy bone,' up my elbow about two inches. A local doctor set it and put it in some sort of aluminum [contraption] around the elbow, then bandaged it. But in working the bone back down, he cut a nerve, which, of course, he wouldn't know as he had no X-ray. The bandage was too tight and if the nerve hadn't been cut, I would have felt pain in a few days. But when he did unwrap the arm three weeks later, halfway from my elbow to my wrist was all sloughed off where the circulation of the blood had been stopped. That is what pulled my wrist down and left me no use of my right hand. My mother took me to the doctor daily for weeks until the arm healed. Then in the spring she took me to Omaha where an operation split the muscle from the wrist up to the elbow, perhaps to lengthen it, letting the wrist straighten out a bit and giving me some minimal use of my right hand and arm the rest of my life. But I have never since been able to straighten out my right wrist or the fingers. Fortunately, I could still ride horses and play sports in my youth. It really doesn't bother me as I can still use the hand for typing—the one-finger hunt-and-peck system—and my forefinger became so strong I could pick up and carry small pieces of luggage or the like." Rather than allow his damaged arm to limit him, Rae adjusted to this adversity as he did to all of life's ups and downs—with optimism and humor. And when anyone would go to shake hands, Rae would always thrust out his left hand without any self-consciousness.

"In the summer of 1921 after eleventh grade, I got a job working on the railroad in what we called the section gang, cutting weeds along the right-of-way, removing old ties from under the rails, and putting in new ones," Rae said as he recounted yet another of his ventures. "Although the government owned them, the railroads controlled personnel even down to the section gang. Since the railroads weren't very happy about the government ownership, the workmen tried to make government operation a failure even at the very lowest level of our section gang. They would take out more ties than just those that were worn out, damaged, or burned, including good ones. Of course, putting in all the new ties was expensive. One section gang even buried some of the new ties they removed. But for my gang, there were mighty few new rails we ever put in place. The workday was ten hours but because the eight-hour day had come into existence, we were paid for eleven hours. I received about $5—mighty good for a high school boy back in 1920. My mother packed me a lunch each day and put it in a gallon paint bucket; as my dad was a painter, we had lots of empty buckets with a tight-fitting lid. It was when I worked on the railroad that I established a very useful habit that has followed me throughout my life. After lunch, I would lie down alongside the track for about a fifteen-minute nap. That type of short break has always done wonders to revive me or give me new energy for the rest of the day. One negative aspect of the railroad work was exposure to creosote used to coat railroad ties. The creosote would burn your hands so we had to wear leather gloves all summer. Occasionally, you might unconsciously wipe perspiration off your forehead or your face and get a real burn if there was any creosote on your gloves. For the first time, I joined a union at the insistence of our foreman. None of us were very well-informed about unionism and couldn't care less about what they were doing, but since the boss thought we ought to belong, we belonged.

"On one occasion, another boy and I bummed a freight train to save our money. We got on when the train stopped for water, and rather than riding in the cars, we rode up on the coal car right behind the engine. Of course, the engineer and the fireman knew we were there so to avoid getting kicked off, we kicked coal down. This helped the fireman who didn't have to do all the work himself. That night, for some reason, I got a headache. When the train came into a town that was a kind of terminal for changing crews and engines, we stopped for a couple of hours. You had to be careful near a town or big yard not to be seen, so you dropped off before you got to the depot. My friend told me that a cup of coffee would help my headache. That was my first ever cup of coffee, and it really did stop my headache. After that I drank coffee frequently. But, it was the first and only time I bummed a ride on a train like the hobos. That was also the end of my two-summer career on the railroad."

4 Inventions and Innovations

Members of the Weimer family continued to explore new ways to earn an income, including Rae's jack-of-all-trades father as he described. "My dad seemed to have learned from his motion-picture days about electricity. He and my brother, Doc, had been playing around with electricity in his little shop in the basement. As a result, Doc and my dad did a lot of house wiring in Mason when electricity came. There was no other particular electrician in town, so they had quite a few jobs wiring houses. The fact that Doc had only one eye probably was a big factor in his turning more to reading and experimenting with electrical gadgetry at home than outdoor activity. Doc and the boy next door rigged up a telegraph system from our two houses using a telegraph key. [In fact], Doc arranged all kinds of little Rube Goldberg things in the basement that could be run by battery. But he needed to obtain batteries. The wall phones of those days required two large batteries about as big around as a Ball fruit jar. Because we didn't want to buy batteries, we would go down to the telephone company and tell them that our phone needed new batteries. We worked that to death by getting the telephone company to give us lots of batteries for that poor telephone!

"Eventually Doc and another boy, who lived about ten blocks away, figured out a wireless system using a telegraph key to communicate back and forth. However, whenever they used it, there would be a click in the telephone and no one in town knew what was causing the clicking. This was shortly before World War I." Someone in the government must have learned of this Rae surmised, "Because when the war started they sent a man out to Mason City . . . and took that equipment and put it in a box and sealed it and forbade anybody to open it until after the war. I don't know whether our name being German prompted that or what. Anyway, at the end of the war the government apparently sent word to the town marshal who came up and broke the seal on the box long after there was any desire to play with that equipment.

"My dad was an extremely innovative man. He built a bean thrasher and could always find ways to do things other people hadn't thought of doing. Because there was no electricity [in many of the homes] and because of the demand for refrigeration, one of his innovations was to create a team to put up ice in the winter. We built a long chute from the creek, up an embankment, to an old icehouse with another chute that went through the icehouse to the other side. On this second chute we fixed a chain in the middle with blocks of wood on it and operated the chain with a gasoline-operated flywheel at the bottom. To cut the ice we used a horse to pull a modified plow across the ice, marking and cutting down about a half inch into the ice. We hired a man or two to then saw the ice into chunks. Using ice pipe poles, we floated the chunks of ice down a channel we made in the creek ice, always working from upstream so there was some current to help float the ice down before we pushed it onto the moving chain. Once the ice caught on the wood blocks, the engine would pull them up the shoot and down the other side to sell to farmers and townspeople. We were really selling a service of cutting the ice and loading it into their wagons, a rather profitable cold-winter enterprise. Our icehouse was deep enough to hold eight layers of ice, which could be used during the summer for our home iceboxes.

"About the time World War I broke out, I found another job for myself working on an ice wagon. There was still no electricity in town, so some man hired me to sell and deliver ice to everybody in town. There were cards people put in their windows near the street with numbers to tell you how big a piece of ice they wanted. I put big cakes of ice into a regular farm wagon pulled by a single horse. Once I got to each house, I could see what size people wanted, so I cut the ice, then weighed it on a scale hanging on the back of the wagon, and kept track in a notebook of how many pounds I delivered to each house. No one locked their doors then, so I would carry the chunk of ice with regular ice tongs, put it in the icebox, and leave. One inauspicious occasion found me at our only doctor's house. His icebox was in the dining room sitting on a beautiful oak floor. They had a pretty large icebox so it took a big piece of ice every time I delivered. Just as I was in front of the icebox and started to swing the big chunk of ice off my shoulder, the ice slipped out of the tongs and landed on the floor on one corner of the chunk, leaving about an inch deep dent in that oak floor. I cleaned up the broken ice, dried the floor, put the rest of the ice in the icebox, pulled a right handy throw rug over the dent, and departed. I never heard a word about it. They probably wondered what in the world put that dent in the floor!

"As I mentioned, my dad was very inventive and handy; he could fix anything. He worked extremely hard at whatever he did, setting a stiff pace for the rest of us. But he never really knew the value of money; if he had money, he would spend it on something, whether he needed it or not."[9] Rae saw his mother as the backbone of the family, as he continued, "My mother was the stabilizer of the family, managing the farm income and the one who encouraged me to attend college."

5 Time for Fun and Games

All was not work for the Weimer boys, as Rae and Doc found ways to have fun, too. In those days you devised your own entertainment—there were few movies, no radio and no television—innovation was necessary. Church events provided many of the small town's social opportunities especially during the holiday season. Even in his youth, Rae displayed his impish sense of humor as an occasional prankster.

"Our Christmas dinner was usually followed by downhill sledding in our pasture with many town folk joining us. Every youngster in that part of the country had to have a sled about the time he was able to sit up," Rae recounted. "Doc and I were no exception and Santa Claus brought us each a sled when we were one and two years old. Before either of us was of school age, we began to hear rumors that there was no Santa Claus. One Christmas Doc and I each received new, larger sleds when we were [around] five or six. It was with those sleds that we trapped my dad into revealing the identity of Santa Claus. Suddenly we asked him one day how much those sleds cost, and he told us. We then said in glee, 'Oh, so Santa Claus didn't bring them, you are Santa Claus!' And that is the way we convinced ourselves that there was no Santa Claus. It was not a disappointment that we had lost Saint Nick, but rather a sense of pride that we trapped him and had solved the mystery.

"[Later], we took those sleds and fastened a wide board on the back. On the front, we bored a hole down through the sled and the board and put a bolt in so the sled could be turned from side to side. Then we put a railing down each side of the sled with handholds in it. That really made a bobsled that would seat six people. We would use [this bobsled] on a hill where we would slide down at night by dim street lights. This was on a dirt road and about halfway down you had to go over the sidewalk crossing, which made a little bump in the road. It was a long walk back up [the hill] so you got a lot of exercise. Everybody had great fun.

"My brother never participated in [the sledding] probably because he didn't see so well at night with only one eye. He lost his eye early in life. One of the things we did was to roll a hoop made from a wheel. We knocked out the spokes leaving just a rim, then we would nail a stick on the bottom semicircle from either a barrel stave or anything that had a little circle to it, and roll the hoop around. Well, Doc stumbled, fell, and punched his eye out with that stick [severely damaging the retina]. In Omaha, a glass eye was fashioned that turned with his other eye making it very hard to detect he even had a glass eye. I vividly remember an incident about seventh or eighth grade before we had a furnace in school; we had only a stove in the middle of the room. After walking to school in below zero degree weather, Doc hung up his coat in the cloak room then walked up to this real hot stove. Suddenly, his glass eye exploded and was blown into a million pieces all over, but didn't cut his eye. Later in life when Doc would have his eyes examined—he had a very good memory—he would memorize the eye chart when he read it with his good eye then read it off from memory for the glass eye. After the doctor wrote down the prescription, Doc would tell him one of his eyes was glass! Doc thought that was very funny.

"Christmas Eve was a big event at the churches in the small Middle West towns. Every youngster in the church and Sunday school took part in a Christmas play. Following the play, Santa Claus would appear. No red suit or white beard seemed to be available, so an adult from the church wore boots or high shoes, a fur coat with the collar up around his face, a stocking cap, a pair of spectacles, and perhaps an artificial beard, not necessarily white, to stick on his face. The youngsters all tried to guess the identity of Santa Claus. One year when I was home from college, I was asked to be Santa. That pretty much baffled the kids since they didn't know me or had not seen me recently; I don't think many adults guessed who I was either. The last event of Christmas Eve was receiving a knit bag with hard candy, an apple, and an orange. That was the only time of year we ever had an orange. Christmas was the only time we had oysters, too. My mother was a member of the First Baptist Church so Doc and I became members when I was eight and he was ten; my dad never belonged to a church, nor did he attend services. The three of us would go to church, come home, light our Christmas tree, and open our gifts. I should mention that [when we still] had no electricity, our Christmas trees were lit with candles.

"Halloween was a fun time but all 'trick' and no 'treat.' Some favorite tricks were tipping over everyone's outdoor privy and sometimes maybe opening the gate and letting the milk cow out. (There were no indoor toilets then.) One year, we got a wagon and not only did we tip over the privies, but we loaded them on this wagon and hauled them downtown and set one in the front door of each store. That really made one of the most amusing sights as people came downtown the next morning and had to move the privies out of the way before they could open the stores. Of course, we had to do this long after midnight to avoid getting caught.

"Along a stream known locally as Muddy Creek, a flour mill was erected. Farther up the creek from the mill was where I learned to swim. It was an all boy's swimming hole, sans bathing suits, and obviously never available for girls. Swimming there was pretty much a sink-or-swim deal in which one might wade along the edge of the creek until someone would think it was time for you to learn to swim, pick you up, throw you out in the middle, and let you swim back. And that is how we all had our swimming lessons. We did fix up a diving board by hollowing out under a large tree and fastening a plank under the roots but extending it out over a small log so it would get some spring and make it possible for us to have a good diving board. As summer temperatures in Nebraska could exceed 100 degrees, we small-fry would hike off to the swimming hole each afternoon to cool off. I guess it was with a great sense of pride that we each learned to swim, dive, and build a sense of comradeship.

"The creek, where we learned to swim, provided ice for great skating parties in the winter. In our version of ice hockey we used any kind of block of wood for a puck. Hockey sticks were either cut from a tree branch that had a curve to it, or made from a buggy stave (there were lots of old buggy tops in those days). If there wasn't any ice on the creek, we took our game to the streets using a condensed milk can and pounded it up and down the street.

"A windmill was used to pump water from a 200-foot well for the cattle. It ran twenty-four hours a day, pumping water into two tanks. When there was insufficient wind blowing, it was necessary to ride out to the farm to start the gasoline engine to pump the water. On Sundays there might be eight of us boys who helped start the engine and would then play hide-and-seek on horseback in the pasture's draws, or gullies. In summer, the day might end with us skinny-dipping in one of the farm's galvanized metal water tanks. Of course, we'd then have to pump more water to replenish what we'd splashed out."[10]

"On Labor Day when I was in seventh grade, my father, brother, and I decided to build a tennis court. There was a large vacant lot of a few hundred feet between our home and our neighbor to the west. Because that land had a slight slope going uphill toward the windmill, we used a team of horses and plow to break the sod. We then used a scraper, sometimes called a slip, to remove dirt and level the field. It was an all-day job for the three of us. From Sears, Roebuck and Montgomery Ward catalogs, we ordered backup and center nets, rackets, and tennis balls. Soon we were in business with the only tennis court in town. It was a joy to have this facility, and I think many other youngsters in town learned to play tennis, just as we did, on our court.

"There isn't much to be said about the social life of Mason City, as I remember it. Our social life largely stemmed from the churches. As I recall, we never went to other people's houses for meals except our relatives,' and no one else came to our house except relatives unless it was a hired man. Instead, the women of the church would get together and serve dinner downtown in the City Hall on election days and other events. There was another event that the whole community and nearby farmers would attend called a 'box social' held in the Opera House with a program of some kind before the box dinners would be auctioned off. Women brought the evening's dinner in a box, which supposedly was wrapped unidentified. Bidding was spirited and amusing. I suspect most wives tipped off their husbands as to the identity of their boxes. For pure devilment, sometimes a friend would bid up the basket to make a husband pay more for his wife's basket. The whole money-raising event for various organizations was great fun and frolic.

"The only dances I recall were barn dances. I did learn to square dance. But I can't recall much dating where you made a date to go somewhere. What you usually did was meet the girl you wanted to walk home after church on Sunday night. Again, we had no cars. I can remember some time in junior high there was one girl, Belle Mulvaney, whom I dreamed of taking someplace. But she lived out in the country and her father wouldn't let her date, although I think once we double dated with another couple. On May Day the boys would take May baskets to the girls, and I remember going out in the country on horseback to deliver a May basket to Belle. The custom was that when you took a girl a May basket, you knocked on the door, and she would run and try to catch you and kiss you. I can't remember if Belle ever took after me to kiss me, but if she did she would have had a tough time catching me on a horse!

"Mason City [eventually] had two theaters with movies shown only on Saturday—a matinee and an evening show. Those were the days of 'serials' such as *The Perils of Pauline.*[11] All the kids in town would be there on a Saturday afternoon. In addition to the serial there was usually a comedy. The Opera House decided to open a [second] movie theater. Because of my dad's experience running a chain of movie houses, he did all the installation and buying of equipment. At first, Dad ran the machine, then taught Doc and me to do it. After that, Doc and I did it every Saturday afternoon and evening. The reason we both worked was the projector had to be constantly cranked. When you had to stop and change reels, there was a gadget on the machine where you ran glass slides that sold some advertising to local merchants. One person ran the slides while the other changed reels, threading the film through the machine by hand. While the advertising slides were shown, a boy would go through the audience selling popcorn, Cracker Jacks, and candy. By the time the Opera House opened their theater, we did have electricity, but since we had no lamps powerful enough to generate sufficient light, we used two long sticks of carbon that came together at a point and made a tremendously hot, white light for the projector. Because of the great fire danger, the movie booth had to be lined with asbestos and the door kept closed, even in summer when it became sweltering. With no air-conditioner and with the door closed, it was murder in there. The longest movie produced at that time (I think it was twelve reels) was *Birth of a Nation.*[12] Needless to say, we didn't have a second show the Saturday we showed that film."

6 School Years

Rae started school later than many of his classmates as he elucidated, "Because my birthday came in November, some two months after the school year started, I was not permitted to enroll when I was two months shy of my sixth birthday. Instead I started school when I was six years, ten months old. And I certainly didn't start with *Sesame Street.*

"When I was in lower grades I, and most of the boys in those days, wore overalls to school. We definitely did not have very fine clothes. Anyway, the overalls had big front pockets handy for carrying a lot of marbles to play with at recess. [Later] I had to shoot left-handed and became adept. By junior high school, our best clothes were knickers; we didn't have any long pants. On one occasion my dad took me and my brother to Grand Island and bought us our first pair of long pants—a salt-and-pepper suit. I hadn't worn it very many times—you always saved your new clothes to wear only on Sunday or some special event—but there came a time when [for some reason] I wore them to school. (My mother wasn't home to see.) Anyway, our desks had an ink bottle receptacle and I was either taking the cork out or had it in my hands when it spilled right in my lap. Well, that made quite a splotch on my light gray pair of pants. I ran home, a couple of blocks, and got out a big crock and some milk. I put the stained part of the pants in the crock, filled it up with milk, and let it soak. Do you know that took every bit of the ink out of those pants? It was a miracle. We had no dry cleaners and my mother would have had to wash, dry, and iron them so they could be worn again. That day might have been labeled life's darkest moment!"

Rae's high school years were busy ones divided between classes, sports, other extracurricular activities, farm chores, and earning extra money.[13] He described his athletic experience. "In ninth grade I went out for football and basketball. Beyond the creamery was a baseball diamond, a half-mile track around the diamond, and a field where we played football.

Other than a roofed grandstand there were no other facilities for the athletes or the fans. At football games, most spectators just lined the side of the field. The track and football athletes had to dress in the basement of the high school before walking, or running, to the field—nearly a mile away. There were never enough boys in high school to make up eleven players for the football team, requiring us to dip down into seventh or eighth grades to pick up more players so we would have at least twelve or thirteen. If you ever saw a ragtag football team, that was us! No two headgears were alike—they certainly were not very good protection. It wasn't until my junior year that we had jerseys all alike but with no numbers. For shoes, we would all find a spare pair and have the shoe shop put some leather cleats on the bottom; I don't believe any of us ever bought a pair of football shoes. My mother was certainly not in favor of my playing football, or football at all for that matter. Doc didn't play any sports and that added fuel to the flame, so she thought it didn't make much sense for me to be risking my life and limb doing such crazy things either.

"On a football trip to Broken Bow, one boy didn't have enough money to pay his train fare; I guess all of us had to raise money to pay our own train fare and the school paid for the hotel. Because we were traveling in cold weather, we all had coats and some blankets, which would go on the floor between facing seats along with all our luggage and football gear. Instead of putting all the football gear there, we let this boy lie on the floor covered with blankets and coats so when the conductor came through the train to gather our tickets he wouldn't see the boy who got a free ride. That trip was my first time staying in a hotel."

Already exposed to, and experienced with, innovative thinking, Rae excelled at the then popular activity of debate. Debating most likely enhanced his persuasive abilities to convince others of his position as well as his skills in listening to another point of view, teamwork, and collaboration that would serve him well later in his career. "When I was in high school, the superintendent initiated a debating program, which I found appealing. There were tryouts for all students who wanted to debate and I made the team. Doc was then a senior, two years ahead of me, and he was on the debate team, too. About two weeks before our first debate, the superintendent hired a college student from Kearney to coach us for those two weeks. We worked diligently during our open periods at school and in the evenings we would give talks and rebuttals. I was the first speaker, followed by a girl named Florence, and Doc was the anchor. Our topic was debating whether the government should own and operate the railroads. Later, we won the county championship debating other towns in our county. Before the state competition, I got tonsillitis and couldn't go so Doc, Florence, and an alternate went but lost in the state contest. I think the debating experience had a strong bearing on my life and helped me to set goals later in life."

Rae described other experiences with public speaking and oration. "Another time I stayed in a hotel, also in Broken Bow, was for the county declamation, or speaking contest. This was a year after I won Mason City's oratorical contest. My mother went with me and saw me win the contest that night, which entitled me to go to the state contest in Scottsbluff. While I don't remember the outcome, I do have two gold medals: one just says 'First Oratorical' and the other says 'First Place Oratorical CCAA.' Another time I won, the first prize was not a medal but $15, which was a lot of money then! We were given a general, broad subject such as railroads or farming; an hour before the contest you would get a specific, narrower title. I found it great fun to prepare by reading about a general subject before giving a ten- to fifteen-minute talk about a narrower, related topic.

"Our basketball trips involved traveling by train from town to town for several nights leaving considerable time on our hands during the day. I do recollect going over to the local courthouse to see if they had a trial going on. I was real fascinated to sit in the courtroom and listen to the trials. That experience prompted me to want to be a lawyer. The experience of the debating team was also a big influence in guiding me in that direction, but I knew I hadn't enough money to attend the university's law school in Lincoln. And because Doc had gone to Kearney, I made up my mind to go to Kearney first, then, if I could see some means, go on to Lincoln to get a law degree. Later, I figured becoming a lawyer would require more time and money than I could afford.

"For several summers I mowed grass for extra cash. With no paved streets and no gutters, grass grew alongside all the streets in town so the city would hire me to use our team of horses pulling our mower to mow that grass. It paid pretty well. They were paying for a team of horses plus a person to do this, which gave me quite a lot of summer work keeping the grass and weeds in check all over town.

"I even worked as a janitor in high school. When two boys in their senior year were graduating, the job was posted. Another boy and I decided we'd put in a bid for the job of $45 per month, which gave us each $22.50. The school board surely got their money's worth out of that meager pay. Our job was to sweep all the classrooms and stairways daily, clean the blackboards, dust the erasers, pick up any trash around, and occasionally wash windows. In the winter we had to remove snow and ice from the sidewalks all the way to the street. Our most difficult job in winter was to fire up the furnace no later than 5:00 a.m. so the classrooms would be warm when the students arrived at 8:00 a.m. In the morning we had to put in fresh coal as well as stoke the furnace during the day. On Saturdays, we had to haul out the ashes. This kept me busy in addition to playing football and basketball and debating. At the beginning of my senior year in high school, the superintendent asked me if I would like to be valedictorian based on my good grades for the first three years of high school. I told him no because of my many extracurricular activities plus my custodial job.

"The end of World War I brought a new holiday to America and a spontaneous celebration throughout the land. I was in high school at the time. When word of an armistice reached the school, the building emptied as if on fire and everyone raced for the center of town. A huge bonfire had been started in the center of the business area and grew to immense proportions as the afternoon faded into night. The wearing of hats and caps was still in style and for some strange reason headgear was snatched off all heads and tossed on the bonfire. People searched the business area and beyond for boxes, crates, or loose lumber—whatever could be found and hauled to the fire. It must have been near midnight before I headed for home. That decision was prompted by a celebrant attempting to toss a wooden box on the fire but, instead, throwing it over the fire, striking me on the head. With a bloody gash, I thought it best to return home.

"Decoration Day on May 30 was the only other holiday that might interrupt school. During my school days in Mason City there were a number of

Civil War veterans still living there, one of them being my grandfather, David Weimer. The program called for patriotic speeches and music. One of the features was for a grandson or granddaughter of a Civil War veteran to recite the Gettysburg Address. My brother did it two years ahead of me and my turn came my senior year in high school in 1922."

After graduating from high school in 1922, Rae would leave Mason City, a town he felt shaped who he was. "As I look back on my early childhood, I am much aware that Mason City offered so very much to me and the other young people in their growth and development. Its very environment, characteristics, and the pioneer spirit of the older inhabitants indoctrinated us with a sense of responsibility, adventure, and opportunities for experimenting and innovation." Little did Rae know as a boy that one day he would join a most experimental and innovative newspaper, then go on to do his own innovation in journalism at the University of Florida.

7 College Years

Entirely new experiences awaited Rae when he moved to the much larger town of Kearney, Nebraska, from his hometown of Mason City, to attend college. "By fall 1922, I had saved enough money from the railroad to buy a new suit of clothes—because the college required coats and ties in class—plus $40 in cash when I enrolled at Kearney State Teachers' College, the only place I could afford to go," Rae said. "Of the thirteen-member 1922 graduating class of Mason City high school, three went to Kearney that fall." When Rae was honored by Kearney State College in 1980 as an outstanding alumnus, he described in his speech his first impressions: "Having thought of myself as a country boy from the hills of Custer County, I found Kearney, with both electricity and pavement, markedly different from Mason City. What a thrill to come to a city and drive on paved streets! As I recall it was nearly fifty miles from Mason City to Kearney and not a foot of paving until we hit Kearney city limits."[14]

Scraping to pay his college expenses, Rae worked numerous jobs throughout his college years and had to scramble to find affordable lodging as he recounted. "Doc had gone to Kearney for two years and arranged a job for me with the superintendent of maintenance for the college. Again, I was on the janitor force working a couple of hours a day Monday through Friday and all day Saturday, earning 30 cents an hour. My accommodations were a rented room in a private home six blocks from the campus. Custodial duties included cleaning gymnasium locker rooms and showers, as well as the pool. Saturdays were largely spent at the girls' dormitory just across the street from the gym. I had to vacuum or mop the reception area and the hallways. When I came down the hallways the girls would shout a warning, 'Man in the hall.' Now that didn't mean for all the girls to rush out to see me—no siree—it meant shut the doors and stay out of sight. Guess that told me something![15] In the winter we had the additional chore of cleaning snow off the sidewalks. Working as a janitor was enough to pay my room rent, about $6 a week. By that time Doc was working on newspapers, first in Nebraska City and then in Omaha, and he would send me $5 or $10 a week, which was the only money I had to buy my meals. My laundry I would send home each week for my mother to wash then she would send it back in the same container. All I had to pay for laundry was the postage to mail it back and forth.

"I enjoyed college that first year, worked very hard at studying (harder than I had ever worked before) and had some pretty demanding professors. Originally Kearney Normal School, later Kearney State Teacher's College, was largely for teachers. Enrollment was about 600 students. I never went to Kearney with any idea of becoming a teacher; I thought I still might be able to become a lawyer. I avoided the education courses instead focusing on history, political science, English, chemistry, and zoology. My history professor really stimulated my interest in that subject. I also relished chemistry so much that, instead of concentrating on course requirements, I spent too much time experimenting."[16]

By the time Rae arrived at Kearney, he was an outgoing and social fellow, engaging in a variety of activities: "My extracurricular activities included freshman editor of the *Blue and Gold*, the college yearbook; editor of the college newspaper, the *Antelope;* temporary secretary of the freshman class; the YMCA; and member of Emanon (Emanon is 'no name' spelled backwards), an all-men's organization providing public speaking experience. I was also chosen for the debate team, a little unusual for a freshman. The Forensic League was organized at Kearney in the spring of 1922, and its first president was my brother; when I started college, I was elected president for my freshman and sophomore years. In my sophomore year, I won the all-campus Blue and Gold popularity contest." Recognized for his excellence in debate and public speaking, Rae was initiated into a forensics honor society at the end of his sophomore year when the Nebraska chapter of Pi Kappa Delta, among the oldest forensics organizations in the United States, was installed at Kearney College in May 1924. He was also chosen president of the Zeta chapter at that time. Participation in forensics and debate honed Rae's critical thinking and public speaking abilities. His curiosity, open-mindedness, and ability to see another's point of view enhanced his success in this pursuit. Rae developed a healthy questioning attitude based on some skepticism and not accepting everything at face value. In later life, he continued to question and to seek knowledge.

Rae was less successful at physical pursuits, as he explained, "Because I wasn't good enough to play varsity football [as a freshman] in Kearney's league, I played on the second team, the one that takes all the beating practicing with the varsity. During one of the three games the second team played against the Industrial School of pretty tough boys, I was carrying the ball, got tackled, and turned completely over, landing on my head. I was knocked out until someone threw water in my face.

"I should mention that my father had given me the nickname of 'Bill,' and sometimes 'Bill Dugan' out of fear that I would be upset being called 'Red' because of my red hair. No one ever called me 'Red' until college, and then I got the nickname quick. When people would see someone with red hair they didn't know, they would just call you 'Red.' In the yearbook listing of the second string football team, my name appears as 'Red' Weimer.

"Some of us formed a new organization at Kearney in my sophomore year that was pretty funny. You would be surprised how many students were redheads or had auburn hair. They all qualified for our new group called 'Order of Pink-haired Sheikhs and Shebas.' There were twenty-five members. An account of the organization of this group is interesting. Our yearbook said, 'The old saw that red hair always covers a cranium filled with dynamite is a lot of baloney, indignantly protested a group of true Titian tint holding a council of war in the lower hall one evening last October. Let's form a club and prove forever and anon that a carrot-colored thatch is not to be laughed at or despised but is "a thing of beauty and a joy forever."' Another paragraph referred to this group as 'Order of Pinks.' Little did they know that those would have been fighting words come the 1940s and 1950s when the 'pinks' would refer to Communists.

"In the summer of 1923, I gave up my room in the rooming house to save money and lived in a tent behind the gymnasium. Alongside the football field was a 'tent city' of three or four large Army tents with wood floors that accommodated at least three cots. We had to use the gym to shower and shave. Once snow piled up all around and on top of the tent in winter, we were pretty insulated. Plus, we had some kind of portable oil-burning stove in the center of the tent along with plenty of comforters and blankets. In contrast, the tent was mighty hot in summer. To earn extra cash, I used an electric iron I had (we did have electricity in the tents) to press clothing for some of the other boys in our 'tent city.'

"Later, a friend and I got a place together living in a local realtor's basement room with two cots. Instead of rent we did chores around the place: mowing the lawn, washing windows, hauling garbage weekly to a hog farm, and, our most difficult job, firing the furnace. The whole family must have bathed in the morning because we had to get up no later than 5:00 a.m. to have the furnace heated for hot water. But firing up furnaces was 'old hat' to me after doing so at home and later in high school." The two young men also set up a short-order restaurant on campus with the equipment owned by the college. They were provided all their food plus 20 cents an hour to run the eatery, as Rae told one interviewer.[17]

"Despite a lack of money to do very much, we did have some social life in college," Rae recalled. "We had a date almost every Sunday night walking girls from their dormitory to the Methodist Church downtown. After church, we shared a Coca-Cola or dish of ice cream at a Greek restaurant, before walking the girls back to the dorm. Other social activities included having a taffy pull in the basement of the dormitory or walking out to a lake for a picnic.

"There were only two fraternities on campus: one was the poor boy's fraternity called the Caledonians, which I joined, and the other adopted Greek letters but was not nationally associated. The latter was largely made up of the town boys and some of the outstanding athletes; it was known to be a rather rowdy, drinking fraternity. The Caledonians never dreamed of having liquor.

"Even our dances had no alcohol or spiked punch. Because none of the dances were on campus and because none of us had cars, we tried to find a hall or other place downtown within walking distance. While I was editor of our college newspaper, the *Antelope,* I got to talking with the dean of women and told her we should have school dances because so many students did not date or found it difficult without an automobile. As a result, the two of us planned to hold an all-school dance in the gymnasium. Of course, to promote the event, I carried the story in the school paper. The dance was a big success; after that dances in the gym were rather frequent.

"Another project I promoted through the *Antelope*, as a member of the Theater Arts League, was to stage *H.M.S. Pinafore* at a lake about a mile up from the college. The music department supplied the singers while the Theater Arts League provided hands to do the building and staging, including building a ship. People sat on the bank around the lake to enjoy this light opera.

"I acquired my first automobile from my most unusual money-making experience. I was always looking for jobs of some kind that would earn me money; the only money I had was what I could earn. One day [during high school], the town banker called me and said he had a job for me helping a tenant on one of the bank's farms. The job was to help this farmer run a still yielding moonshine for the banker's own supply. After I had gone to college, I would come home only at Thanksgiving and Christmas. The last year I was in college and home for Christmas, the banker called me and said he had something he wanted to give me. He seemed happy with what I had done for him and gave me a secondhand, four-cylinder Buick roadster he apparently repossessed from a debtor who owed the bank money. That was the first automobile I ever owned, ill-gotten as it was."

Rae delighted in his three years of college. Although financial circumstances prevented Rae from completing college, he worked hard there to earn enough money each term—cleaning the boiler room of the girl's dormitory and running the college newspaper. In Rae's view, attending college was a great privilege. He went to college to learn. Coming from a little town in Nebraska, Rae held teachers in high esteem and never wanted to miss a lecture or class. Reflecting on his college days, Rae told one interviewer, "I liked college. I liked learning. After you work on newspapers awhile, you see where you'd like to know more, especially after interviewing people who had better formal educations than you."[18]

Although Rae's views and opinions would get him fired from the college newspaper, he was always true to his beliefs and his right to express them as well as to others' right to express their ideas. His inquisitive mind led him to question everything; he became a scholar through self-education despite his lack of a college diploma. And so, by a twist of financial fate, Rae moved on to his career in journalism in which he would gain renown.

PART II

A Plethora of Papers

8 The Budding Newspaperman

From the small towns of Nebraska, Rae moved on to larger cities. He worked at several newspapers throughout the Midwest gaining experience and moving up to higher levels of responsibility. But his first journalistic experience came during junior high school when he acquired a paper route in Mason City. Rae explained how this came about: "The *Grand Island Independent,* a daily paper, had established paper delivery routes in all the little towns [in central Nebraska]. I got the job of delivering the [paper] in Mason City. [The papers] would come up from Grand Island about 5:30 in the evening and I would be there to meet the train. I didn't have a bicycle, so I usually delivered them in a little wagon I had to haul them around. It would have been much easier and better if I had a bicycle as a youngster, but I never did own one. I can remember many times walking those three miles [from the farm] to get back into town to meet the train after working at the farm all day. The paper cost the subscribers 10 cents a week and I got half of that—5 cents. I worked the route up to about ninety subscribers. In those days I could do that after school and in the winter, of course, the delivery was all after dark. Pulling that little wagon around through snow was not the most pleasant thing, but it made it possible for me to earn most of the money for my clothes and gave me some spending money I wouldn't have had otherwise.

"There was a local paper in Mason City called *The Transcript.* One of the staff had a son my age and in my class. In junior high school we decided to get out our own newspaper. The two of us would go down to the print shop at night when nobody else was there and set type. In those days the type for the paper was all set by hand; there were no linotype machines. So we would take various sizes of type and get on the floor to press by hand the type for printing our paper. We didn't use very small type as was used for most of the news because larger type filled up a page quicker and was the only kind you could hand press on the ink roller, then on the paper. As I recall we got out one or two mighty primitive editions. The copy we passed around at school was mostly hearsay, gossip, and what we thought was funny to say about some of our friends. Little did I know then that that was the beginning of my journalism career. It wasn't a very auspicious start I must say! I suspect if that paper were to come out today, we would probably be sued for libel.

"In high school, an English class project established the first school paper, the *Magnet,* and I became editor. We wrote little tidbits about the school, athletics, and whatever we could. We sent it over to Kearney to be printed. It ended up being tabloid size and four pages. That was my third venture into journalism."

Doc, Rae's brother, had a tremendous positive influence on Rae's newspaper career. Not only were the brothers very close, but Doc preceded Rae in many of the positions Rae would later hold in his life. "At times Doc might suggest stories I should do or critique copy I shared with him," Rae recalled. "By my second quarter in college at Nebraska State Teachers College at Kearney, I had somehow gotten a job as editor of the college paper, the *Antelope,* paying $5 a week, raised to $30 a month in my second year. Perhaps, I got the job because Doc had been editor of the *Antelope* before me. Soon, I learned that I didn't know much about editing a college paper, having been editor of my high school paper for only a couple of issues. As editor, I did a bit of everything: writing, editing, layout, and arranging for the printing. Our business manager, Clay Doggett, also earned $5 a week. The paper was entirely dependent on advertising revenue; as a result, about 75 percent of the space was given over to advertising. Because we were always searching for ways to make a few extra bucks, we thought we would put out a special edition of the *Antelope.* The only money we made was based on the advertising Clay would sell; the paper itself was delivered free. This was not a regular edition, so whatever money we made after we paid for the printing, we divided between us. The 1923–24 year was quite an outstanding one for the *Antelope.* We had reduced the advertising space to about one quarter of the paper. In a national competition among college papers, our September 28, 1923, issue won first place.

"When I went to Kearney, one of the advisors assigned to me was A. L. Phillips, head of the English department, who was also the advisor to the *Antelope* and hired the staff for the paper, including me as editor.

Since I found Phillips of no help with the paper, I became close friends with Ralph Noyer [director of the Extension and Publicity Division], an aggressive thinker who knew the value of publicity and how to get your story told to those we wanted to hear it. As a result, I went to Noyer for most all advice regarding the *Antelope.* I believe Phillips resented the fact that I never came to him for advice about the paper but always went to Noyer. One day Phillips came up to the *Antelope* office with a girl in tow and said he wanted to introduce the new editor of the *Antelope* to me. That was quite a shock; I had no warning it was coming although I wasn't surprised. (Incidentally, I found out later that after I left college, Ralph Noyer was named chairman of the committee responsible for the paper.)

"Later, when Doc and I were working for Scripps-Howard, I learned their practice was very much like Phillips's approach. Scripps-Howard would hire a troubleshooter who would come into town, call the editor on the phone, and ask him to come over to his hotel room. When the current editor would arrive, the troubleshooter would introduce him to the new editor. And this happened all along the line on the papers where I worked, although never to me directly. This happened to Doc while he was editor of the *Columbus Citizen* after he endorsed some local candidates the owner, Roy Howard, did not approve of, and Doc was out.

"Along with my junior class picture in the 1925 college yearbook are my extracurricular activities for that year: Theater Arts League, Forensic League, YMCA, Spanish Club, 'Pink-haired Sheikhs and Shebas' and Pi Kappa Delta. Beneath that is a description that turned out to be prophetic for how my life turned out. It read, 'What greater crime than loss of time?' Years later as I was retiring as dean of the College of Journalism and Communications, an editorial written by Professor Buddy Davis for the *Communigator* in January 1968 had this in it: 'Who is Rae Weimer? He is a fellow who furiously drives himself, and others, on the theory God put men on earth to accomplish tasks—not swig Budweiser on the patio.'[1] I think it was a nice description of me and almost seemed to answer the prophecy of 1925."

As Thomas Kirwan put it (based on his interviews with Rae), "Stripped of his student editorship, he became convinced that he was destined to be a newspaperman and could learn little about his intended profession at Kearney."[2]

9 The Rambling Years

Spanning fifteen years, Rae worked for eleven newspapers, mostly across the Midwest. It was a golden era of newspapers when he and Doc began their journalism careers in the 1920s. Newspaper giants like William Randolph Hearst, Joseph Pulitzer, and Edward Scripps were purchasing and merging big-city newspapers causing circulation to jump dramatically both in large cities and in smaller communities. Then the Depression hit, bringing a huge drop in advertising revenue for the papers. As a result, papers folded, wages shrank, and staff were let go. These events had their impact on the brothers as well.

Like Rae, Doc lacked sufficient funds to complete college in Kearney. In the fall of 1923, Doc began working at the *Marion Star* in Marion, Ohio, close to the woman he would later marry, Lillian Marston, his childhood sweetheart from Mason City. Rae explained, "Doc had saved enough money, or thought he had, to go back to college as he had finished only two years. He enrolled at Wooster College [Ohio] in 1924, where Lillian was in school, but found out he did not have enough money after all. He went to college during the day and clerked in the local hotel at night. By the end of the semester in early 1925, he was exhausted, almost had a nervous breakdown, and had to return home. Following her graduation from Wooster College in spring 1925, Lillian taught school near Metamora [Ohio] for the next two or three years."

Despite lacking sufficient funds to complete their college educations, in 1925 the Weimer brothers acquired enough money to purchase a struggling publication using funds borrowed from the bank in Mason City. "On Doc's way home from Wooster, Ohio, he stopped by Kearney to tell me he found a newspaper for sale in North Platte that he was going to buy and wanted me to join him. This came just as I had been relieved of my duties as editor of the *Antelope,* cutting significantly into my income, so I agreed to go in with him. Very suddenly, I left college and went to North Platte, about 100 miles northeast of Kearney. We were young and not too bright. When we arrived, we discovered the *North Platte Herald* had been owned by a farmers' union that was losing money and just wanted to get rid of it. After about two months we received several past-due bills. In addition, we weren't making much headway competing with the *North Platte Telegraph*, especially selling advertising, which was damn tough. Everywhere we went, we were turned down. To top it off, the foreman of our composing room had a brother with a private print shop; we suspected the foreman of giving his brother our supplies that had been disappearing. Without much hope of succeeding, we locked the door one Saturday night, packed our trunk, strapped it on the back of my Buick Roadster (the one I acquired as a result of my moonshine job years ago when I was in high school), left a blank check signed to the girl reporter so she would get paid, and drove as far as York, Nebraska, about 200 miles from North Platte.

"Knowing York had a daily paper, we thought we might apply for jobs there. But while eating breakfast, we bought a copy of the York paper to get a feel for what it was like, and there was a headline that said, 'Weimer Brothers Disappear' with a half-column story about our disappearing from North Platte without leaving word to anybody and a review of our six-month tenure there. Deciding it was best to keep going, we drove on to Lincoln, went through Omaha, and crossed through Council Bluffs to Atlantic Isle where we spent the next night. We decided if we left the state there wasn't much danger anyone was going to subpoena us to come back and pay off the debt.

"The next day we drove to Des Moines, Iowa, where Doc got a copy desk job with the *Des Moines Register.* I gained experience reading copy on a metropolitan paper when one of the copy readers threw some my way. But during the day, I was answering classified ads trying to find a job. Finally, I found one selling advertising for ink blotters. After selling only a couple, I discovered I wasn't a very good salesman. Doc and I were putting advertisements in small dailies and weeklies with broad enough descriptions that either one of us might answer the ads; if we got an answer, either one of us might accept the job. We probably overstated our qualifications, at least mine.

"I found an ad for what they called a 'news butcher'—a man who rides passenger trains selling newspapers, candy, fruit, cookies, paperbacks, and other items. Since many of the trains in those days had no diners, people would buy snacks. My job was on the fabled Rock Island Railroad with the run from Des Moines to Chicago." Shortly thereafter, Rae drove to Moline, Illinois, seeking a job there as a reporter. He explained what happened next, "Halfway to Moline, I twisted off an axle on my Buick right in front of a garage facing the railroad track. So I bought a ticket to Davenport where I made application to two newspapers without success. From Davenport, I rode a streetcar to Moline only to find out the city editor of the *Rock Island Argus,* also had no openings. Without finding a job, I took a train back to Des Moines.

"A few days later, a wire from Paragould, Arkansas, replied to one of our ads with an immediate opening for an editor with the afternoon daily. I accepted the position, but it didn't take me long to realize this was a bigger job than I had anticipated—certainly more than I was probably prepared to handle by myself. The job involved getting out a daily, five days a week, as well as a semiweekly and a farm publication three times a week.

"The job in Paragould lasted two or three months before Doc wired me saying he had accepted a job offer for me at the *Moline Dispatch.* Needless to say, I returned to Moline, checked into the YMCA, right beside the paper, and went to work for the *Moline Dispatch.* For several weeks I had general assignments such as covering city hall, the school, and the health office. One of my interviews was with the president of the John Deere Plow Company. Although I wasn't very experienced interviewing people and didn't have sense enough to ask questions, the president gave me a lot of information to write a good story. It was a delightful experience.

"My next assignment with the *Moline Dispatch* was to work in the Rock Island office going through carbons of all the local stories to enable me to write what I thought would be of interest in Moline. I stayed there quite a long time until Doc wired me again to the effect that 'have better job for you here, come as soon as you can.' Doc had left the *Des Moines Register* to return to the *Marion Star* [in Marion, Ohio], where he had previously worked. Thinking I would be able to earn more money, I resigned at the *Moline Dispatch* where I was earning $25 a week. I moved in with Doc, who had a room in a private home, and went to work as a reporter. To my surprise, when I got my first paycheck, it was only

$22.50. When I told Doc it wasn't as much money as I was getting in Moline, he said, 'Oh, I thought you were getting $20 in Moline and this would be a raise for you.'

"Soon I was assigned an interesting job as state editor [for the *Marion Star*] covering several outlying communities in the area. I enjoyed the four to six weeks I spent in each county seat personally training the correspondents so that they could carry on after I left, a new field for the *Star* that increased circulation. A particularly eventful assignment for the *Star* was in Mount Gilead, county seat of Morrow County, where I was to cover all the news in that community and county. The theory was I could pack the paper with Morrow County news for a few weeks before the paper sent circulation people out to sell subscriptions to the paper by showing a sample of all their local news (county fairs, sulky races, picnics, and other local stories) in the *Marion Star*. It was great fun meeting so many people. While staying in Mount Gilead, I often ate in a restaurant that had a pool table and actually played pool with Jim Thorpe, Olympic Gold medalist and one of the greatest Native American athletes this country ever had.[3] He certainly was as good at shooting pool as he was an athlete; on occasion he could run the table without ever missing. When you played with him you always lost, but he was a real nice guy and I had fun playing pool with him. In contrast to my experience with Thorpe, Dick Dunkel, our sports editor at the *Marion Star*, wrote a story about local legend Jim Thorpe that was not complimentary. In retaliation, Thorpe met Dunkel somewhere, smacked him, and broke his nose."

Rae found it quite exciting to cover his first murder story while in Mount Gilead. Provoked by a boundary argument, a farmer shot his neighbor. The prosecutor took Rae along with him to the jail for the interview with the perpetrator. As Rae told the story, "The prosecutor became a good friend but also liked to have his name in the paper, so he wanted me to know what he was doing. Another time he took me on a raid of a still and even gave me a little revolver, maybe a .22, with a wooden handle and short barrel. We had to tramp through the woods and lay in wait all night, but no one ever showed up.

"While I was in Mount Gilead, several young men, who had previously played football in high school, wanted to form a semipro football team. This part of the country was very football-minded as pro football was founded in Canton, Ohio." A group of men, including legendary all-around athlete and football star Jim Thorpe, held a meeting on August 20, 1920, that led to the formation of the American Professional Football Conference (APFC), precursor of the National Football League.[4] "At any rate, these young men wanted me to organize their semipro team," Rae continued. "For the few months I was in Mount Gilead, I served as the coach and mostly general manager, scheduled their games, and handled their money, which didn't amount to much. Every afternoon when they finished work, we held a practice behind the building where my office was; I had a lot of fun with this group of young men.

"After working a few months in Mount Gilead, I was sent to Galion, then Bucyrus, Upper Sandusky, and finally to Marysville. I had done this circuit about a year when Doc brought me into the office in Marion. There, I worked as a reporter covering the courthouse and the railroads. Another assignment was to attend a different church every Sunday and write a story on the sermon. I guess that was one reason that I never affiliated with, or went to, any one church because I had to cover all of them. I found my greatest returns came from careful organization of those who worked for me and in the personal contacts I made throughout my district. Both bore unexpected returns as the lessons learned proved valuable in similar jobs, but on a larger scale, in Fort Wayne and Akron in later years.

"Marion was nationally known as the center for the manufacture of steam shovels, used widely in road work and major excavation such as strip mining. More steam shovels were made in Marion than anywhere else in the United States." In fact, Marion was known as the "city that built the Panama Canal" when the federal government turned to the Marion Steam Shovel Company to supply the shovels for digging the Panama Canal.[5] As steam power declined in popularity, the company changed its name to the Marion Power Shovel Company. Other well-known projects included the Hoover Dam, the Holland Tunnel, and building the launch pad transporters for the Apollo rockets and later the space shuttles for NASA.

Ever peripatetic, the Weimer brothers moved on once again in 1926: "In the spring, Doc was offered a job as editor of the *Olean Herald* in Olean, New York. I left the *Marion Star* within a month or two when

Doc wired me the *Olean Herald* needed a city editor and a sports editor. Olean was a beautiful small city close to New York's southern border with Pennsylvania. Near the Allegheny River, the Allegheny National Forest, and the Enchanted Mountains of western New York, Olean had exceptionally attractive surroundings and climate. I remember writing a regular sports column under the byline of 'Bill Dugan,' which had been my childhood nickname from my dad."

Weimer related to Tom Kirwan in an interview how the *Olean Herald* would cover prize fights. "You would announce it from the window of your newspaper office. You'd get a whole crowd . . . in the street and you'd announce the fight. The fight results would come in by telegraph, but you held back a little so that you could get all the fight in an extra [copy of the paper]. By the time you announced the last of the fight, you went out and started selling the paper. That lasted right down through the early 1930s when radio came and killed it."[6]

"We worked through the summer and into the fall when Doc had a disagreement with the owner of the *Olean Herald* who knew nothing about running a newspaper and had preconceived ideas that clashed with Doc's approach," Rae said of his brother. "Anyway, he fired Doc, but didn't fire me. It took Doc only a week to line up a job in Logansport, Indiana, as managing editor of the *Logansport Press.* Before Doc actually left Olean, rumor around town was that the two of us were thinking of starting another paper. The owner was stupid enough to think the rumor was true and he fired me as well. The sports column I had written was already in the composing room so before I left, I went into the composing room, picked up the copy of my column, tore it up, then got my last paycheck.

"In Logansport [1927], I immediately began looking for a job while Doc and I lived in a hotel overlooking the Wabash River. My job search encompassed Fort Wayne where my application was accepted but I wasn't hired. About a week later, they notified me that a job was now available. As a result, I went to work at the *Fort Wayne Journal Gazette,* a morning paper in competition with the afternoon *News-Sentinel.* My work as state editor was largely at night. I was responsible for news coverage and handling of all stories originating in Indiana, more responsibility than I'd ever had before. In the meantime, Doc had left Logansport for Ann

Arbor, Michigan, where he worked a short time before moving on to Toledo to join the Scripps-Howard chain as news editor on the *News-Bee.* During one of my vacations while working at the *Journal Gazette,* I did some sightseeing in Indiana that took me to Indianapolis. While I was there, I called on three newspapers and told one of the managing editors that I might be interested in a job in Indianapolis someday.

"At some point while I was working in Fort Wayne, I met the society editor of Akron's *Beacon Journal,* named Arletta Schmuck. Because we both went to work around 6:00 p.m., in the summer we teamed up and started visiting some of northeastern Indiana's lake resorts. We would rent a car, drive out, and swim. Some of the lakes even had a chute of some kind you climbed up and slid down into the water. There wasn't much else to do in town and I knew no one. Later she and I bought a publication called *This Week* in Fort Wayne. It was sort of like a magazine of what was going on that week in the city and carried advertising for stores but mostly for movies and other entertainment. About midway through my stay in Fort Wayne, I found the job of working on *This Week* in the daytime and the paper at night overwhelming. A previous stomach ailment recurred as well, sending me to a famous internist in Fort Wayne who advised me there was nothing wrong with my digestive system, but I would have to give up working on a desk job. He said if I didn't work more outdoors at physical labor, I wouldn't live more than two years. (Well, that was in 1928, and this is 1988!) I suggested to Arletta that we sell the magazine, which she did not want to do, thinking we could eventually make money.

"Meanwhile, I received a call from the editor I had spoken to previously in Indianapolis when I visited on vacation, saying he had a desk job open on the Scripps-Howard paper. Thinking this opportunity and change would benefit my health and provide a solution to getting rid of the magazine, I accepted my first position with Scripps-Howard newspapers [on the *Indianapolis Times*]. I told Arletta she could have the magazine; she finally did dispose of it in the spring. The only profit we received from the magazine was a due bill from the Coronado Hotel in St. Louis for some advertising. That August 1928, Arletta and I were married at an Episcopal church in Indianapolis; our honeymoon was a two-week trip to St. Louis where we used that due bill at the Coronado

Hotel. We had to go by bus as we still had no car. Well, the bus had a flat tire requiring all the passengers to pile out into the hot sun until they changed the tire—very romantic!"

During Rae's very short time with the *Indianapolis Times,* the paper won the 1928 Pulitzer Prize for its exposé on political corruption in the state, specifically the Ku Klux Klan. As early as 1924, the paper was dedicated to exposing the Ku Klux Klan and its influence on politics. The *Times* published a series of articles in 1927 revealing corruption between Governor Ed Jackson and Indiana Grand Dragon D. C. Stephenson, which earned the paper its Pulitzer Prize for "exposing political corruption in Indiana, prosecuting the guilty, and bringing about a more wholesome state of affairs in civil government." As a result, the Klan's strength in Indiana was considerably weakened.[7] The *Indianapolis Times* was known for courageous journalism, frequently engaging in crusades against injustice and corruption.[8] The Scripps-Howard papers in general represented the common man and supported the unions, a position that appealed to Rae and may have influenced his decision to later join an experimental newspaper with similar views in New York City, *PM.*

"I enjoyed my tenure at the *Times,*" Rae remembered. "It provided me a lot more experience than I had before, particularly on the copy desk. Another young man and I would read manuscripts for the Bobbs-Merrill printing company to recommend to the publishers whether the manuscripts were worth publishing. I believe we received $40 for each manuscript we read. Another responsibility was to get the final edition out." After only a few months with the *Times,* a serendipity birthday greeting would lead to a new job for Rae.

10 Akron Years

Fortuitous circumstances brought Rae to Akron, Ohio, as he recounted: "In the fall [of 1928], and I have no idea what prompted me to look through some papers, I came across the name of Doc Kerr, who was managing editor of the paper at Marion when I worked there. I happened to note in one of my little calendars that his birthday was coming up, so I sent him a birthday card. Only three or four days later, I received a telegram from him offering me a position on the *Akron Beacon Journal.* The job sounded better than the one I had at the *Indianapolis Times,* so I accepted. However, when I got off the train in Akron, I had a sinking feeling. It was a dirty-looking city when I first saw it. Still, the new job, as state editor, would pay me more as well as give me a chance to do something different. In addition, I had an assistant and must have had about a hundred correspondents in fifteen counties surrounding Akron reporting to me.

"Work started at 5:00 a.m. when I would pick up the mail from all the correspondents. My job was to go through the letters, get them edited and laid out in the composing room before the rest of the staff arrived. Although most of the copy arrived by mail, some stories had to be telephoned in, and I had to write them. First, I had to have my copy set for an early edition of the paper; setting copy for my two pages was a lot of copy to handle. Generally, I finished around 11:00 or noon. I then took the office car to go out and get acquainted with my correspondents. As a result, I spent considerable time on the road. In addition to meeting with correspondents, I toured my district, calling on church, civic, and school groups in the many towns and cities. For the next three years on the *Akron Beacon Journal,* I was assistant city editor, handling all copy except sports and state news. My duties included a number of special editions in connection with the building and launching of the two Akron-built Navy airships.

"Arletta arrived [in Akron] a few days after I did. In the afternoons we looked for a place to live. We found a private home about ten blocks from the office where we had a room and bath upstairs. As I was walking back and forth to work, I noticed an apartment house under construction right across the street and immediately made a reservation. It was a few months before we moved into the only apartment we could afford, which ended up being a kind of sub-basement—half above ground and half below. Arletta soon got a job at the YWCA before being offered a job as society editor for the *Akron Beacon Journal.* She did well there and then the other Akron paper, the *Akron Times-Press,* a Scripps-Howard paper, offered her a job as women's editor.

"By the fall of 1928, Doc had become news editor of the *Cleveland Press,* [while his wife] Lillian was still teaching at Metamora, not far from Toledo where Doc had previously worked on the Scripps-Howard paper there. They married that December 1928. The following summer, Doc, Lillian, Arletta, and I scheduled our vacations at the same time and drove out to Nebraska to visit my mother. Although it was like hometown for Lillian, Arletta had never been to that part of the country. I don't think she very much enjoyed that trip and certainly was not used to the kind of life we had in Nebraska.

"Let me say that Arletta probably was one of the best all-around newspaper women I ever knew. She was a good administrator, a better than average writer, but her forte was in organizing the women's departments and the personnel. She did so well at the *Akron Times-Press* that after a couple of years, Scripps-Howard sent her to Buffalo where the paper was in trouble. From there she later became women's editor of the *Miami Herald,* the *Washington Post,* and the *Chicago Tribune.* As I said, she was such an outstanding newspaper woman and was in such great demand that I think she found more satisfaction as a professional than as a housewife. I must be honest and say that my own background of moving from place to place as better opportunities came up certainly did not do much for a marriage. We did not live together much but didn't do anything about our situation until several years later when she was in Miami and I had gone to New York.

"Akron turned out to be an interesting city. This was also the time of prohibition. Along with prohibition, dozens of speakeasies popped up around Akron, many on the numerous lakes outside Akron. We all carried around a pack of cards, almost like a deck of playing cards, which would admit you to the various speakeasies. Many were near golf courses and served excellent food. I not only enjoyed the speakeasies but got passes to play golf from the newspaper. Before prohibition ended, we used to have office parties and make our own gin. We would buy alcohol in gallon cans, then buy juniper drops at the drug store to mix with distilled water to make the gin. We soon found out that tap water was just as good and cheaper.

"Incidentally, the *Akron Beacon Journal* was owned by C. L. Knight [whose family business would become the Knight Ridder media company bought out by McClatchy in 2006]. C. L. would write editorials now and then, always in longhand, and there was only one operator in the composing room who could read his writing to set his editorials. Most interesting about C. L. was that he loved to have a picnic out at his farm and invite an agnostic or atheist along with a person of faith. I remember one Sunday he had Clarence Darrow, a Catholic priest, and a Jewish rabbi as guests. After the picnic, C. L. loved to get them into discussions and arguments, a very enlightening spectacle for the rest of us lucky enough to get invited. He didn't invite many of the staff, but if you pleased him, and he liked you, you got invited back. These experiences offered wonderful food and a most interesting afternoon listening to people discuss politics, religion, or whatever he could get his guests started on.

"I suppose the most significant event that happened while I was working on the *Akron Beacon Journal*, was the market crash of October 1929. Akron was, of course, the rubber capital of the world where all the tires and other rubber products were made by Goodyear, B.F. Goodrich, Firestone, General Tire, Seiberling, and other smaller manufacturers. During the Depression it was so tough in Akron that no one was buying tires, and the rubber industry practically collapsed. No money was in circulation and it wasn't long until all the schools paid off the teachers in scrip. The newspaper also paid us in scrip. I was getting $60 a week at the time of the crash, then had a series of pay cuts that brought my salary to $46 a week before I had to accept scrip. I would take part of that scrip and deposit it at the Rathskeller Restaurant allowing me to eat lunch until it was gone and I was told I needed to give them another piece of scrip. Or, I would go to one of the department stores and buy something that might cost $2.50. By giving them a piece of $5 scrip, I could get back change in cash. That was the only way Arletta and I could keep our life insurance intact because the insurance company would not accept scrip. Also, you could spend your scrip at the department stores and they, in turn, would give it back to the newspaper to pay for advertising. Unfortunately, the scrip wasn't any good outside Akron.

"During the Depression, there were apple sellers on every corner. Men and women would get a box of apples and stand on the street corner to sell the apples in an effort to make a little money. Goodwill Industries established a remarkably smart plan by selling tickets for their soup kitchen. Those of us who had a job, would buy these tickets from Goodwill and then, when a panhandler would ask for a dime (you suspected he might buy a drink with it), you would hand him a ticket that entitled him to get a bowl of soup from Goodwill Industries.

"One of the most exciting events during my Akron days that led to lots of newspaper stories involved the Goodyear-Zeppelin Corporation's entry into the field of rigid airships. The first airship they built was the *Akron.* Steel was too heavy so a new, lightweight, age-hardened aluminum alloy, called duralumin, was employed to add greater strength to the airship. Helium fuel was so expensive, it was not routinely vented; instead, they caught water vapor from the exhaust in a bag inside the airship, which required a generous supply of water for ballast. This way the airship didn't lose weight as it burned fuel during flight.

"When the *Akron* was nearing completion, Goodyear-Zeppelin's publicity department drove up to Cleveland to get Lawrence Tibbett, a famous baritone opera singer who performed over 500 times with the Metropolitan Opera in New York City, and I went along. Back in Akron, I was able to join Tibbett's walking tour up in the airship's catwalks and interior. My other direct experience with the airship was during the christening. Of course, the airship belonged to the Navy and the general practice when they christen a ship is to break a bottle of champagne over the bow. That wasn't possible with the airship, so they decided to put forty-eight racing pigeons in a crate inside the nose at the bow of the *Akron.* Mrs. Hoover came out from Washington to do the christening on a scorching hot

August day in 1931. Many of the women in attendance wore white summer dresses. The pigeons had been put inside the night before, and the next afternoon when Mrs. Hoover pulled the cord to release the birds, not only did the birds fly out, but dirt and droppings came down on the honored guests right below the bow. It was a mess! We newspaper reporters thought it awfully funny, but I'm sure the guests did not.

"The *Akron* made a number of flights from the Goodyear hangar, a building about as long as a football field. This was the biggest attraction at the time in Akron; we all went out to see the airship take off and especially to see the complicated landing maneuver. The airship couldn't land except when the wind was no more than a few miles per hour at ground level. A dolly, or crane-like device, run by a motor was used to catch the nose of the airship. Meanwhile, men on the ground would grab ropes that dropped down in order to steady the airship as it maneuvered in to hook on to the dolly, which would then pull the airship back into the hangar."

Both the *Akron* and sister airship, the *Macon,* were among the largest flying objects ever built. They were designed by the Navy for aerial scouting missions and carried several airplanes inside. Because the United States had a monopoly on helium resources, unlike Europe, which had no helium resources, America could use the safer helium in their airships rather than the highly flammable hydrogen. Rae recalled, "In 1933 off the coast of New Jersey the *Akron* broke apart in a storm and crashed into the sea with only three survivors out of the seventy-six people aboard. The crash of the *Akron* was a tremendous story in town. I remember receiving a call about 2:00 a.m. asking staff to come to work to get out extra editions the day the USS *Akron* crashed in the Atlantic. [The *Macon* was also lost at sea in 1935 off the northern coast of California with all but two individuals rescued, the Navy's last rigid airship and the last to be built in America.[9]] After that, Goodyear branched out and began building blimps—non-rigid airships with no internal structural framework—that used helium Goodyear was able to get from the government.

"Ward Van Ornam, engineer and inventor, was also one of the world's premier balloonists at that time and an employee of Goodyear. He won five National Balloon races. Initially, the balloon sport was hot-air balloons, and Akron had many balloon races. One time, I was fortunate to ride in one of the helium-filled balloons with Clyde Schetter who also worked for Goodyear and was one of the understudies for Van Ornam.

"In 1933 we were back off scrip but my original salary was not restored. So, when the editor of the *Akron Times-Press,* a Scripps-Howard paper, offered me a job as assistant city editor for $60 a week the following year, I jumped at the chance. After about a year there, I became news editor for the rest of my time at the *Akron Times-Press.* My jobs included heading the copy desk in the final preparation of all copy in the paper. In addition, I supervised the sports, women's, and city departments in their writing and editing as well as supervising the makeup of the paper and the making of pictures into zinc cuts for printing. Two years into my time with this newspaper, I staged one of the largest model plane building contests ever staged in any place. For the finals, witnessed by some 200,000 people, we combined the model contest with a giant air show at Akron's municipal airport.

"This change in jobs was how I came to meet Ruth Meister. Walter Morrow, who was then editor of the *Akron Times-Press,* was one of the real outstanding editors who came out of Oklahoma. Ruth worked as society editor for him on the *Oklahoma City Times.* Eventually, that paper closed and was sold to the more powerful *Daily Oklahoman,* a morning paper, and she joined their staff. Walt, a real innovator and aggressive editor, wanted a new society editor on his Akron newspaper. Instead of the society editor they had, who was hired for her 'society' connections, Walt wanted a newspaper woman with more actual newspaper experience. He called Ruth, asking her to become society editor of the *Akron Times-Press* in the summer of 1937, which was when I first met her." Ruth received her bachelor's degree from the University of Oklahoma in 1931. After spending a year at home, she began her newspaper career as assistant society editor (1932), then society editor (1934–37) for the *Oklahoma City Times.* In 1936, Ruth traveled by ocean liner to Europe for the Olympics in Berlin.

"In those days it was not uncommon for wealthy families to sponsor stars in the opera," Rae continued. "Frank Seiberling, president of the Seiberling Rubber Company in Akron, sponsored a young soprano from the Metropolitan Opera in New York. Every year when the opera closed in New York, it went on tour. The first place it went from New York City was to Cleveland because they had a large auditorium seating thousands of people and making it lucrative for the opera. I got a call from the *Akron Times-Press* managing editor asking me to take Ruth to the opera in Cleveland where this soprano, sponsored by Frank Seiberling, was going to star. I think he called me because, first, it was my day off and he wouldn't have to send someone on company time, and second, because I had a tuxedo! Consequently, I took Ruth to the opera—it was the first time I had ever been to an opera. Afterward, she went backstage to interview the diva for a story in the *Akron Times-Press.* That was how we met." Ruth recalled Rae's courtship noting that Rae was asked to drive her to Cleveland to cover an opera, "I don't know if he really wanted to go," she said.[10] Fortunately for both Rae and Ruth, this event played a pivotal role in their lives.

As editor of the *Akron Times-Press,* Walt Morrow imparted his wisdom as Rae recalled. "Walt Morrow was an outstanding newspaper man who taught me a great deal. As news editor, all the copy that went into the paper, except sports and society, went through my hands. But I was responsible for both the sports and society pages getting in on time. One day there was an error in the paper and Walt came stomping out of his office, waving a newspaper, and storming about something he didn't like, before tromping back into his office. Less than ten minutes later, he called me up to his office and said: 'Rae, I want to tell you something right now. Someday you are going to be a great newspaper man, but I want you to learn one thing: When there is something wrong in the paper and I raise hell about it and tell you about it, I want you to then forget it and don't carry it home with you. Because of the many problems that you have on a newspaper every day, don't carry those problems home and worry about them at night. After the paper comes out, that is the end of it. Learn from your mistakes but don't worry about them at night. Come back the next day with a fresh mind for a new day.' Well, that was a great lesson to learn because being concerned about my responsibilities at the paper, I might very well have gone home and worried about him being mad about something in the paper. I have never forgotten his advice in the many years since."

Scripps sold the *Akron Times-Press* in 1938 to the *Akron Beacon Journal,* ending both Rae's and Ruth's time with the paper. Ruth returned to Oklahoma City to work for the Oklahoma Publishing Company

(OPUBCO), which had combined their morning and evening women's staffs; she was hired as society editor and assistant women's editor for the *Times* and *Oklahoman.* Rae would move on to another Scripps-Howard newspaper in Buffalo, New York.

11 Moving On

Rae's next assignment with the Scripps-Howard chain led to influential connections and relationships that furthered his newspaper career. "In the summer of 1938, Scripps-Howard was making an all-out effort to win a place for themselves in Buffalo, and I think they already knew they were going to fold up the *Times-Press* in Akron," Rae recounted. "They sent me to their Buffalo, New York, paper, the *Buffalo Times,* as assistant city editor, but because of a staff shortage, I also did a great deal of writing as well as attending civic gatherings or business luncheons and dinners. At many of these events I spoke, sometimes about the paper, other times about various civic campaigns under way in the city. I made all of the assignments for reporters and photographers and directed not only our coverage of news stories, but also had charge of many promotion stunts. These included athletic contests, poster and story writing contests in the schools, and the making and showing of motion pictures of special events. Scripps-Howard brought in staff from their other papers including George Lyon from the *World Telegram* as managing editor and John Lewis from Colorado. (Both men would work with me later on *PM* in New York.) I had never been on a paper where there was more innovation to help the *Times* succeed. Our competition was the morning paper, the *Courier Express,* as well as the afternoon paper, the *Buffalo News.*"

Along with the rise of unionization during the Great Depression, newspaper guilds were forming in the 1930s not only to increase journalists' wages but also to improve their working conditions. Yet, some journalists felt it demeaning to join a union or worried about their job security if they did join. When Rae went to Buffalo he said, "None of the papers had a guild. But, as newspaper guilds were spreading across the country, the *Buffalo Times* staff began to organize a guild. Some of the staff had pretty wild ideas of what demands they would make; a group of us who were more conservative outvoted them to prevent the guild from being too radical. As a result of my group's influence, we held an election to choose someone to attend the national convention in San Francisco; I was one of those elected. On our train journey to San Francisco, we stopped in Ogden, Utah, where a telegram caught up with us saying, 'The paper folded tonight. Go on to the convention and have a good time' signed 'the Staff.' So, that was the end of the *Buffalo Times.* George Lyon went back to New York while John Lewis went to work in Cleveland for the Scripps-Howard Feature Service. Because of the reputation I made in Buffalo and in Akron for Scripps-Howard, they immediately transferred me to another of their papers in Cleveland, the *Cleveland Press.* Lewis and I were the only two members of the editorial staff placed by Scripps-Howard when they folded the *Buffalo Times.* I ended up working on the copy desk of the *Cleveland Press* [until early 1940], where Doc had worked some years before.

"From the *Cleveland Press,* Scripps-Howard had sent my brother, Doc, to Columbus, Ohio, as managing editor of the *Columbus Citizen.* By that time, he and Lillian had two young children. They lived in the suburbs for maybe a year before buying a farm of about 400 acres six miles east of Columbus. With three houses on the property, Doc and Lillian were able to move my mother and dad to the farm. My dad did a lot of work around the farm as Doc was working all the time either at the *Columbus Citizen* or in an advertising agency.

"After working several years at the *Columbus Citizen,* Doc had endorsed some candidates for local elections that Roy Howard [head of Scripps-Howard papers] in New York did not approve of so Doc got his call to come over to a hotel to meet his successor. That was one of the difficulties of working for Scripps-Howard. Roy Howard thought he knew more than anybody else and called signals from New York that didn't make much sense on the local papers. After Doc was fired as editor of the *Columbus Citizen,* he formed a public relations and advertising agency in Columbus, the Weimer Organization, which I would later join. The offices of the Weimer Organization were in the Ohio National Bank Building. This bank had five other banks in Ohio, and their account was our bread-and-butter account.

"Another account was the Buckeye Aluminum Company in Wooster, Ohio, that had some production troubles. The president hired us, a public relations firm, to work internally with the employees. We decided we'd publish a newsletter, a little newspaper. So each month we traveled the 100 miles northeast of Columbus to Wooster. There, we would focus on one department with photos of the employees showing all the different jobs they did to turn out the product. We emphasized how skilled they were at their jobs, hoping they would live up to the praise. After a few months we had raised the efficiency of that plant about 25 percent.

"In 1948 we organized fundraising in Ohio for the American Heart Association's first big national campaign. My job was to visit every county seat to visit the head of the medical association or a leading doctor in town to get him to assume responsibility for organizing a local fundraising committee. Doc was very public-minded. He helped colleges combine their fundraising campaigns so businesses were not constantly bothered by different colleges asking for money. He also gave his time during World War II to raise money for the war effort."

12 What a Newspaperman Does

During his many years of newspaper experience, Rae had a variety of duties as he described: "A desk editor, or as I was called in my day, the news editor, is the traffic controller of the newsroom. The greatest pressure of planning, editing, critiquing, and juggling each day's news copy, falls on the desk editor. Today, he sits at a computer terminal, his eyes riveted on a screen as the day's news copy flows through the terminal. A news editor must know what else is going on in the newsroom—what local stories are in the making; what state, national, and world stories are pouring in over the wire services; and what the photo possibilities are for these stories. He has to remember what stories he has already placed on what pages in order to remake pages for late-breaking news and photos. Throughout all of this, he must design the pages to be attractive, quickly appealing to the reader's eye.

"As assistant managing editor [later] at *PM,* I did everything there was to getting out a newspaper. I was responsible for the production, selection and editing of all material, stories, pictures, and cartoons in the paper. I laid out each day's paper, deciding on picture and workspace—I had to decide on each department's space. To do this, I had to work with each department editor to determine what stories they would feature, what art went with each story, and what angles were most important to be stressed. Part of this process was deciding which stories would be told in words versus which ones would be told in pictures. Other responsibilities included all editorial expenses, purchases and budgeting, and assisting with guild negotiations.

"I was not an 'inner office' editor but worked 'on the floor' with the staff where I could keep my hand on the pulse of the paper. That, and the ability to call signals quickly, made it possible to take a story late in the afternoon and suddenly turn it into a major 'takeout' of five to ten pages and still go to press by 10:30 at night. Knowing how to work with people and organize a staff to obtain maximum effort from them was one of my strengths.

"Beyond the paper itself, I worked with the promotion and circulation departments on campaigns for selling the paper. Campaigns included posters, movie shorts, radio programs, mail campaigns, city and community surveys, and speaker groups. Our speaker groups might focus on luncheons for radio commentators with our foreign correspondents and writers when they returned from abroad. Similarly, I discussed with our syndicate manager the resale of our features throughout the world. For this editorial staff of nearly 200 individuals, I was responsible for checking and approving all purchases, expense accounts, and pay for overtime."

In the fifteen years between 1925 and 1940, Rae worked for eleven newspapers in six states, some for only a few months, others for several years. Most of the time he was an editor, but he started out on the copy desk or reporting, working his way up to positions with increasing responsibility and scope. A number of these traditional newspapers went out of business; however, Rae also moved on for better pay and influence. His last newspaper experience would be for a radically different newspaper and would last eight years. The job would also be the culmination of his newspaper career as he joined the revolutionary and historic, but short-lived, *PM* newspaper in New York City in 1940.

PART III

PM—A Pioneer Publication

13 The Visionary Ralph Ingersoll

Rae Weimer felt fortunate to be a part of the radical publication *PM*, providing the following background about its founder. "Ralph Ingersoll was a flamboyant editor and a literary genius in publications. He was a sensation in New York in the 1920s and 1930s when, at age twenty-five, he helped establish the *New Yorker* magazine. It is almost ironic that Ralph studied mine engineering at Yale before taking a job as a gold miner in California in 1921. He gave that up shortly and became a reporter for the *New Yorker* magazine, and only a year later was its managing editor. At age thirty, he brought financial success as managing editor to *Fortune* as that publication was struggling for survival, by attracting a great number of outstanding writers and establishing its reputation. [Ingersoll's] crowning glory of success probably was as publisher of *Time* magazine. While [Ingersoll] was establishing *Time*, he designed the format and content for *Life* magazine. When *Life* burst on the scene in 1936, Ralph thought he should have been named publisher, but instead, Henry Luce, the American magazine magnate who founded *Fortune*, *Time*, and *Life*, took that job for himself and offered Ralph a million dollars a year to continue as publisher of *Time*. Ralph turned Luce down. Disappointed about seeing credit for his creation of a new magazine go to someone else, Ralph then set about planning for his own newspaper. Ingersoll was determined he would not work for anybody else but have his own newspaper. He set about formulating plans for his creation, founding *PM* before his thirty-ninth birthday."

As Ralph Ingersoll conceived of a revolutionary concept in newspapers, World War II had begun in Europe. Most people in the United States were isolationists as were newspapers at that time. Although there were still a dozen newspapers in New York City, those lacking sufficient advertising revenue failed or merged. Ingersoll proposed a newspaper without advertising to ensure companies did not influence what he published; he wanted to insulate his publication from interests detrimental to the truth, such as advertisers, financial backers, and politicians. He espoused a liberal philosophy supporting workers, unions, minorities, and those oppressed. The journalism climate in New York City at the time did not favor the success of his radical ideals. No paper was more widely anticipated than Ingersoll's dream, nor has there probably been more written about any publication than was written about *PM*. What follows will detail Rae Weimer's role in this experiment, from his perspective, which would profoundly influence his later career trajectory.

"First, Ingersoll returned to his Connecticut farm," Rae said, "where he dictated a sixty-one-page 'Proposition to Invent a Daily Newspaper' which became *PM*'s prospectus—a great document and the most famous and widely quoted newspaper prospectus in the history of American journalism. In part, Ingersoll issued his prospectus as a basis for raising money. First, he promised a 'complete newspaper,' edited as if no other newspaper were being published. Ralph wanted his new newspaper to have various departments for all classifications of news. He thought he could succeed by having the best writers, expressing public opinion ideas, and using a permanent research staff like the one that helped establish *Fortune*. The prospectus held that headlines would not be written to fit the space, but to tell the story. And they would be written by the writers. Writers would be supreme—no mutilators on a copy desk to ruin their copy. Ralph thought he would combine photographs with words to cover the newsbeats as he had done with *Life*. But little did he know the problems of putting all this together in a daily publication when he had been accustomed to weekly publications.

"This neophyte publication was in a whirlpool of controversy before it even had a name. When Ingersoll first conceived his paper's dummy format, he called it 'Newspaper,' and the first mock-up carried that title. At that time all the newspapers in New York were sold at newsstands, not home delivery, so his theory was that when people asked for a newspaper, Ingersoll's 'Newspaper' would be handed to them. Not a very good idea."

The exact origin of the name, *PM*, is unknown but explanations abound. Rae recalled, "As our promotion campaign progressed, city newspapers began to take stock. Columnists frequently referred to it 'as that new pm,' meaning a new afternoon paper in contrast to 'am' for morning papers. One biographer credited Lillian Hellman [a close friend of Ralph Ingersoll's] with suggesting the name to him. I believe the name was generally established by columnists, although Ms. Hellman may have been the one who convinced Ralph to use it. A common practice in New York was to refer to the morning papers as the 'AMs' and the afternoon papers as the 'PMs.' Since this paper was planned for an afternoon paper, it was referred to as 'that new PM.' We all decided then, that because of all the publicity in New York about this 'new PM,' we would adopt the name. In adopting the name, *PM,* our lawyers discovered a house organ in New Jersey at a small manufacturing plant that was called PM; we had to send somebody over to buy it to kill the name and avoid a lawsuit when we used it."

Ingersoll's outline for his new type of paper was filled with idealism, compassion, seeking the truth, and a commitment to improve the way people live. Part of his prospectus read as follows: "We are against people who push other people around . . . We are against fraud and deceit and greed and cruelty and we will seek to expose their practitioners . . . We respect intelligence, sound accomplishment, open-mindedness, religious tolerance. We do not believe all mankind's problems are now being solved successfully by any existing social order . . . , and we propose to crusade for those who seek constructively to improve the way men live together. We are American and we prefer democracy to any other principle of government."

"Pretty high-sounding goals but difficult, I suspect, to fulfill all of them," Rae continued. "The one statement that really characterized *PM,* if any one thing did, and sort of became our motto was, 'We are against people who push other people around.'

"There is no question of where *PM* stood on political issues. We were liberal but made it clear to readers we were without political affiliation. Truth is hard to come by, but *PM* tried to live up to its policy that said, '*PM* is in business to tell as much of the truth as it can find out because it believes journalism's function in a democracy is to see truth in contemporary life and to print it without fear or favor.' Another section of our policy said, 'What makes *PM* tick is a serious belief in honest journalism as an end in itself—the bringing of the truth to the people so that they may decide for themselves what to do about it.' Ingersoll was a visionary, an idealist to be sure, but not always a practical publisher. The goal of journalism to him was to serve the truth and to pursue a better mankind as he expressed: 'The world is better off for knowing the truth although truth is difficult to discover. It takes intelligence, character, perseverance, and energy to achieve. It is worth all these things—it is worth the service of a man's life.'"

Marshall Field III, *PM*'s primary financial backer, also expressed his view of *PM*'s approach to the news, which is ever relevant today: "*PM* comes to its conception of news with the conviction that the world of economics, politics, and international affairs has become at once so dangerous and so complex that the ordinary man cannot find his way around in it without warnings and aids. Hence, *PM*'s emphasis on 'debunking' current news stories—'debunking' being journalese for the scalpel dissection of the interested motives which certain power groups may have in propagandizing a given version of the news."[1]

"Ingersoll drew heavily on his magazine experience in many of the innovations for his new paper," Rae explained. "He shook up the conventional American press with revolutionary techniques in reporting, writing, layout, art, and photography. We pioneered in use of ink that did not rub off on your hands, wider columns and larger type, and a completely departmentalized paper, all for better readership. We were trailblazers with our use of maps. Three of our staff mapped the war like nobody did—nobody.[2] These techniques, all revolutionary to the American press, brought concern to our immediate competitors, and set the pattern for change in succeeding years [in the newspaper business]. But Ingersoll had no idea of the difficulties he would have implementing all of his ideas in a daily publication when he had been accustomed to weekly publications."

14 Launching *PM*

Undertaking this journalism experiment required financing. Rae expounded on how money was raised to launch *PM:* "With his blueprint in hand and a reputation as a boy wonder in publications, Ingersoll went out to raise money. Contacting his millionaire friends to invest, he raised $1.5 million from sixteen individuals whose names read like a list from Dun & Bradstreet. He gave his investors no promises or commitments for a return on their investment. [Among the initial investors were heir to the Marshall Field department store fortune, Marshall Field III; A&P heir Huntington Hartford III; John Deere heir Dwight Deere Wiman; Sears, Roebuck heir Marian Stern; Philip K. Wrigley, son of the founder of Wrigley's gum; Elinor Gimbel, a progressive women's rights activist, who was married to the grandson of the founder of Gimbel's department store; and investment bankers among others.] I saw a copy of the contract, which gave Ingersoll sole power to do everything the way he wanted with no strings attached. A good, seasoned newspaper man would have advised against trying to launch a new paper in New York's highly competitive market of eleven other daily papers with only a million and a half dollars. But Ingersoll, if he was so advised, was undaunted. I also worked with the promotion department in the greatest advertising and promotion campaign ever put on for a newspaper. No publication ever came into being with so much advance publicity and public comment as did *PM*. About a third of the money was spent in promoting the paper before it ever hit the streets.

"Controversy built up about *PM* before it ever became a reality when Ingersoll announced his new paper would carry no advertising. The other newspapers saw that if a newspaper without advertising succeeded, it might cause a great deal of damage to their way of doing business. I believe Nelson Poynter, editor of his father's paper, the *St. Petersburg Times*, was partially responsible for this idea." Poynter and Ingersoll shared a liberal philosophy supporting good government, minority rights, and independent journalism. According to biographer Roy Hoopes, Ingersoll was introduced to Poynter through a mutual acquaintance. From his own experience, Poynter had become convinced that he could publish a profitable newspaper without conventional features or advertising and had drawn up his own prospectus for a paper based on his ideas. Initially, Ingersoll and Poynter hit it off based on a mutually shared vision. Ingersoll wanted Poynter to take over the business side only of running a newspaper but became annoyed after Poynter described the venture as being run by "Ingersoll and Poynter," resulting in unkind words going back and forth between the two. That was the end of any potential partnership.[3]

Because of Rae's previous affiliation with the *Buffalo Times* as well as with the first two editors Ingersoll hired for his unconventional newspaper, these two editors recommended Rae to *PM*'s founder as Rae recounted: "About the time I was working for the *Cleveland Press,* Ralph Ingersoll had left *Time* and was working on plans to start his own newspaper in New York City. One of the first people he hired to help him get organized was George Lyon as managing editor; Ralph would be editor. George decided to call John Lewis in Cleveland and ask him to join the staff as top assistant managing editor. [Shortly thereafter] George called me about joining *PM.*"

Rae told Thomas Kirwan in a phone interview that John Lewis said to George Lyon, "George, we'll never get a paper out without a copy desk—it's just impossible. So that's when they called for me to come down from Cleveland as assistant managing editor. There had never been anything like it, before or since . . . *PM* was challenging—the innovation of the century.[4] We had people far beyond New York City excited about this new paper, and that excited me, too. Here was something different and I hadn't run into anything like it in my career.[5] I certainly had a liberal point of view but it was more conservative than Ingersoll's. I had to adapt myself to a certain extent. We were an upstart, noisy, rambunctious newspaper and not very many people liked us. Every newspaper in town disliked us. We founded the paper on the basis of giving a voice to those groups that didn't have one.[6]

"The experience for me was unlimited in going to New York, although having grown up in Nebraska, New York seemed like a long way away.

As I began working on newspapers in the Middle West, I had the idea that the best newspapers were published in New York, that the best newspaper men were in New York, and that New York newspapers were the cream of the crop. So, when I got the invitation to join *PM,* it was with some apprehension that I accepted. I really didn't know whether I was qualified to take over a top position on a paper like *PM*. But George Lyon and John Lewis had both supervised my work in Buffalo, and John had seen the kind of work I did in Cleveland. They assured me that they wanted me, that I was the person they needed.

"Once I got into the swing of New York journalism, I found it not that much different than my previous experiences. I soon discovered that New York reporters were not any better than the reporters out in the hinterlands. Some, of course, were excellent writers, but they didn't know how to report and dig into a story in depth the way we did in the smaller cities. The reporters were not as thorough as those out in Ohio, Indiana, or on smaller papers where we worked the stories harder; we drained them dry to get all the facts about our stories. In New York, there was so much news that a big story one day would be forgotten the next. I soon gained a great deal of confidence in myself—I did know what I was doing."

15 Stellar Staff

Ingersoll's promotion of the first new daily New York newspaper in twenty years created such excitement that no fewer than 10,000 applicants sought positions with *PM* for only 150 jobs. *PM*'s own subscription promotion, the new *Picture Magazine Daily* (May 20, 1940), reported the new paper was already promising "the most brilliant editorial staff ever gathered together by one newspaper." Ingersoll boasted that his paper would be published and written by the most talented writers available and the best newspapermen in the country. Later his own memos indicated those he hired did not live up to this ideal: Every newspaper man in America seemed to want to quit his job to come to work for a paper that said it would believe in the members of its staff. Many of the original staff of *PM,* supposedly "hand-picked," were hardly even looked over; they simply battered down the doors and came to work. The editors and assistant editors, who were there to weed them out, were overwhelmed.[7]

"I was not one of the applicants but was directly recruited by *PM* staff, although I must say I was quite excited at the prospect of going to work in New York," Rae said. [Rae was drawn by the liberal stance of Ingersoll's vision in fighting for the underdog. In Akron, Rae had seen "unfairness to a lot of people who were in trouble.[8]] "I arrived six weeks before the first edition of *PM,*" Rae remembered, "to help whip together a staff, already hired, that had many specialists but cried out for a few real hard-headed newspapermen. As I looked at the staff Ralph first hired, I thought he erred in his choice of 'good' writers. Ralph would hire people from the field he wanted them to cover: a teacher to lead the education department or someone active in the labor movement to be labor editor, for example. In fact, the teacher knew nothing about reporting or covering news; the labor editor could not even type and was useless in trying to cover a labor story. In the first three months, about half of the initial staff was gone.

"George Lyon saw early on that *PM* needed to have seasoned newspaper people, which is why he called John Lewis to come down from Cleveland and a month later asked me to join him. Ralph originally thought copy readers spoiled a reporter's copy. Well, Lyon, Lewis, and I decided we had to have a copy desk; reporters couldn't edit their own copy. In fact, very few [individuals] can write copy that is not improved by a good copy reader. So, one of my primary responsibilities was to put in a copy desk. All the copy was to flow through me to the copy desk, and I would assign what we wanted done with it. After that, copy would come back through me to go to the composing room. My first task was to bring on some staff from the *Buffalo Times* including two copy editors, a sports editor, and a couple of reporters. When you have a big news front to cover, it is always helpful to have people you know and can depend on.

"As I mentioned, I hired all the copyboys, all of whom were college educated—either a college graduate or in the last year of college. I guess this was my first experience teaching journalism. I was very fond of those kids. Once a week I would get them together to explain why we did this and why we did that, how we got a particular story, and then answer any questions they had. My goal was to instill what a newspaper was all about from an editorial point of view." John Lewis described to Tom Kirwan how Weimer became the newsroom's teacher both at the *Buffalo Times* previously and now at *PM*; he helped the rookies learn their trade and helped seasoned writers refine their writing for a newspaper.[9] The paper and its staff mentored numerous talented, creative, and public-spirited journalists, many of whom later shaped American thought.

"Most of the staff were young," Rae continued, "Our staff was made up pretty much of young people, perhaps because older, established journalists were less likely to risk giving up security to join such a controversial paper, an experiment by all standards. [However, some of the older, seasoned staff took pay cuts to be given free rein in pursuit of their own dreams.] Due to the war and the draft, I suspect our staff turned over several times before the war ended. Yet, there were many well-known writers, cartoonists, photographers, and outstanding newspaper men of their day who joined *PM* at various points. Those who say *PM* lacked talent in its staff have not examined the facts, in my opinion. I think we had the best photographers, the best artists, and as good a staff of writers as any paper."

The staff of *PM* included renowned authors, photographers, cartoonists, and more. Most of these illustrious figures would stay but a short time at *PM,* with the exception of I. F. Stone and Max Lerner who continued until the end. People who worked at *PM* at some time (although many only briefly or as occasional guest writers) included such other well-known figures as Lillian Hellman, Dashiell Hammett, Dorothy Parker, Ben Hecht, Erskine Caldwell, Walter Winchell, Dalton Trumbo, Margaret Bourke-White, Ernest Hemingway, Donald Ogden Stewart, James Thurber, Crockett Johnson, Leo Huberman, James Wechsler, Benjamin Spock, Ted Geisel (Dr. Seuss), Elizabeth Hawes, Hodding Carter III, Penn Kimball, and Pulitzer Prize–winner Edna Ferber.[10]

What follows are Rae's impressions of some of the outstanding staff who worked for *PM.* "One was Alexander Uhl who gained his reputation as a war correspondent in the Spanish Civil War. Uhl was the foreign editor at *PM,* covering the European theater during World War II and was awarded the French Legion of Honor. Bill Walton was a *PM* reporter after working for the Associated Press; he was the first reporter to parachute into France during the invasion of Europe. After the war, he came back as a reporter for *PM* and was also a close friend of John F. Kennedy.

"Ingersoll had the idea that Dash [Dashiell Hammett] could improve the staff's writing, so he hired Dash to sit alongside me, as all the copy that went into the paper came through my hands, except sports. Dash was such a good writer and had a quiet wit, but after a few months, I think Dash got bored with the task (as did I), and left." When interviewed by Paul Milkman, Rae recounted that Hammett was conducting anonymous last-minute editing to improve the prose style of the copy after it had already cleared the copy desk, a process Rae thought foolish.[11]

Lillian Hellman, the famous American playwright, had an interesting association with *PM,* Rae recalled. "She had invested money in *PM* and was a close friend of Ralph [Ingersoll]. Hellman was romantically involved with Dash; Ralph was also enamored of Lillian. A story has been told that one night she invited both men to her country home out in Long Island and announced she had chosen Dash over Ralph. Brokenhearted, I guess, Ralph began to give his attention to creating *PM* and gave up on a romantic relationship with Lillian. But in the early days of *PM* we had staff meetings and dinner at Ralph's apartment every

Friday night—just the editors, not the reporters. Lillian, as far as I can remember, was always at those meetings. I guess while she chose Dash over Ralph, she and Ralph remained good friends. After dinner, Ralph and Lillian would go to the theater while the staff stayed in his apartment for several hours playing poker before we went home.

"Mayor of New York, Fiorello LaGuardia, was one of New York's more colorful mayors and an extrovert. At one time when all the newspapers except *PM* went on strike, Fiorello would go on the city's radio station Sunday morning to read the comics to children; his reading was much funnier than if you had read the comics yourself. He agreed to write a column for us in the latter years of *PM*. His chauffeur would drive him over every Friday afternoon, then Fiorello would bring his column to the composing room and hand it to me in person, wait for me to read it, see if I had any comments or questions, and then he would leave.

"I. F. (Izzy) Stone, one of the better-known Washington reporters, before and after *PM*, was on our Washington staff. He knew Washington better than anyone and could obtain material people wanted kept under wraps." Stone stopped attending briefings in Washington when he developed hearing problems, diligently reading the public record instead.[12] Rae recounted to biographer Myra MacPherson how Stone sometimes used his hearing loss as a ploy such as when Stone did not respond to a question Rae asked him: "If he didn't want to hear you, he pretended you weren't around. So, I dropped a one-dollar bill and said, 'Izzy you dropped some money on the floor.' And he went right for it."[13] After the war, he did a piece on the Jewish diaspora from Poland to Palestine by following the dangerous route the Jews took, but his popular series boosted circulation only a fraction. Early on, someone suggested he change his name, Isidor Feinstein, to minimize his Jewish heritage so his reporting would be better received. According to Myra MacPherson, because "stone" is "stein" in German, he kept the Isidor, used only the initial *F*, and added the last name "Stone" to become I. F. Stone, referring to himself as "Izzy" in 1937. MacPherson quoted Stone as saying, "It was just about the time of our third baby and I thought in part if he had a neutral-sounding name maybe it would save him some trouble."[14] In contrast to some who found Stone demanding, temperamental, or humorless, Rae described him differently: "Izzy was one of the most gentle, kindly people, besides being an extremely good reporter. . . . Izzy was very accommodating. If I asked him to do something, he never argued with you. He might tell you it couldn't be done, but he said it quietly. A very popular guy, everybody loved him."[15]

"Widely syndicated columnist Max Lerner's first newspaper job was with *PM*," Rae recounted. "Although he had already established his literary reputation [through his articles, reviews, and political editorship of the magazine *The Nation*], he had no knowledge of, or background in, working on a newspaper. A very liberal writer and thinker as well as a good lecturer, he came to work for us in 1943 writing editorials. Max and I would meet in the morning to decide the topic of his editorial. Then he'd have to catch a plane for a speaking engagement an hour later and would begin writing his editorial during the flight. At the plane's first stop, Max would telegraph me a page through Western Union. At the next stop, he might be driven to his next address, continue writing while en route, give another radio address, then cable the conclusion of his column from there. I had a hell of a time putting it all together in the right order. In the early days of the paper, we changed deadlines often and changed from an afternoon paper to a morning paper. Max had difficulty keeping up with deadlines for his editorial. One night he was a little later than usual. Well, typically there is a newspaper practice of blanking out space for an advertisement when copy is late for the first edition with the statement: 'Reserved for Macy's or Sears, etc.' That night I had the editorial page proof prepared with a statement in the middle of the blank page, 'Reserved for Max Lerner' and gave the proof to him for checking. I think it took him days to recover." Max Lerner said of Weimer, "You taught me the ropes . . . You taught me what a good newspaperman does and is."[16] Lerner said of the new paper and of his new boss, "It was probably the most innovative paper in the twentieth century, certainly the most innovative after the 1920s. Rae was the stabilizing force and, more importantly, made the innovations work. I was taken with Rae's professionalism and competence."[17] Rae and Max Lerner continued a friendship for the rest of their lives.

"The famous author of children's books, Dr. Seuss, was hired to draw our editorial page cartoons," Rae recalled. "Ted Geisel, his real name, was a marvelous person: unassuming with a pleasant personality, he would try to produce anything you wanted. I regret not retrieving some of his more than 400 cartoons when *PM* folded; they would be priceless today." His editorial cartoons made Fascists like "Hitler, Mussolini, and Tojo look like forerunners of his book *How the Grinch Stole Christmas*."[18] Geisel also developed a project to learn what his friends disliked about *PM*. The study was so successful, Ingersoll noted that about half of the "original enemies of *PM*" began to read the paper consistently. A tabulation opinion sheet was devised with staff encouraged to conduct a similar study among their friends.[19]

"James Thurber, known for both his writing and his cartoons, contributed drawings to *PM*," Rae said. "As his eyesight was failing [from sympathetic ophthalmia], he had to use a large sheet of paper, about 10 by 14 inches, which we would then reduce down to a size we could print.

"One of the more famous staff at the beginning of *PM* was Margaret Bourke-White, undoubtedly the most famous woman photographer in America. When she went out on a story, she usually carried five cameras. The reporters almost ran to hide when they knew we were sending Margaret Bourke-White out on a story because the reporter who accompanied her had to help carry her gear. She worked for us probably less than a year. As I recall, we were paying her about $12,500 a year, but she was too expensive for us to keep. Part of the expense was running her film through the darkroom as much as her salary." Bourke-White left *Life* briefly in 1940 to work for *PM*, staying only four months before returning to *Life*.[20]

Rae illuminated the role Walter Winchell played at *PM*: "Surreptitiously, the influential gossip columnist and radio commentator, Walter Winchell, wrote a column for *PM* occasionally. In 1940 when Wendell Willkie ran against Roosevelt as he sought a third term, Winchell was writing a column for the ultraconservative Hearst newspapers supporting Willkie. *PM* was strongly in support of Roosevelt, the liberal [who had supported *PM* since its inception], and so was Winchell personally. He offered to write the column and we accepted. We called the column "Willkie Buttons by WW." Now both Winchell and Willkie shared the same initials—W. W.—which confused the public as the column was anti-Willkie. Nobody knew who wrote the column except for, I suspect, only a few of us in the office. Winchell's inimitable style of poking fun was very amusing. Winchell also did a Sunday night radio broadcast that bordered on libel, so his sponsor retained legal counsel to review his draft. He would then call me at home before I left for the office and give me the items the lawyers struck out. Monday morning, we'd carry a box on the front page saying, 'Here is what Winchell couldn't say on the radio last night.' Our circulation might jump by 10,000 to 15,000 with all the readers wanting to find out the spicy part Winchell was prevented from broadcasting.

"The last person I want to mention was a freelance photographer by the name of Arthur (Usher) Fellig who used the trade name 'Weegee.' [He earned his name by always appearing first at major crime scenes, as if a Ouija board had directed him to the spot.] Because we were a good market for the itinerant peddler of both foreign and domestic pictures, Weegee gravitated to us rather early in our publishing. He dropped into our Brooklyn office one evening with his most recent photographs, which we immediately bought, and he became a regular caller. In fact, he was around so often that, despite our large photography staff, we began to give him regular assignments. Weegee had a great feeling for what made an appealing photo. He was unlike your typical reporter covering an event like a fire, for example. While the other reporters were shooting photos of the fire, Weegee would turn around and take pictures of crowds gaping open-mouthed at the fire or of what the firemen were doing, making a great human interest story. He greatly enjoyed his job and although he chased police and firemen or documented on film the sometimes seamy side of life, he always focused on human interest stories in New York City. Some of his works were even collected by the Museum of Modern Art and exhibited in 1943."

A long-standing contributor to *PM* was pioneer photojournalist Mary Morris. One of the first female photographers in journalism, she worked for the Associated Press before joining *PM* at its inception to provide pieces for the Sunday issue. Her photographs appeared in numerous magazines; later she was renowned for her photographs of Hollywood's biggest stars.

Well-known humorist Frank Sullivan and Rae became friends when Sullivan wrote occasional columns for *PM* during World War II. He had worked for the *World* until 1931 when it ceased publication. Known as a prolific letter writer, Sullivan penned the following in a letter to Rae dated July 20, 1945, expressing his gratitude for the chance to contribute to the paper: "If I may be quite serious, I would like to say that being on *PM* is, and has been, a hell of a tonic to me. It is like being on *The World* again . . . *PM* is at the threshold of a career that might well be as brilliant as *The World*'s was. The fun is only beginning. *PM* will really come into its own in the post-war years when it will be needed even more than it has been the past five years."

Sullivan was most noted for his annual holiday poem, "Greetings, Friends!" published in the *New Yorker* from 1932 until 1974. In his "pome," as he called it, he wrote witticisms about his New York friends and famous people of the day. Rae and Ruth were included in the December 23, 1944, poem with the lines:

> Love from this intrepid rhymer
> To Mr. and Mrs. Rae O. Weimer . . .

Much was made about *PM* both favoring and hiring Communists. In fact, the Communist unions were against *PM* as interventionist and the anti-Communist unions were down on *PM* because it was smeared by enemies as "red."[21] Rae's response to the criticism was, "Yes, there were Communists on the staff, but I am confident there were not many. To those contemporary writers who say part of *PM*'s failure was due to conflict between Communists and anti-Communists on the staff, I say poppycock. All of the copy in the daily paper went through my hands and only one writer seemed to have a bit of bias occasionally in his copy." Painting its staff as Communist tainted Rae Weimer as well. In later years after he had retired from the University of Florida, he related to writer Lisa Barr in 1993 that when he arrived at the University of Florida in 1949, he was greeted by a red-baiting editorial in the *Jacksonville Times Press* about how another "pink" was coming to teach at Florida. Rae said, "That dig hurt."[22]

16 A Rocky Year

Before the first year of publication ended, *PM* was in trouble. Overhyped, the publication did not live up to its publicity, promises, or prospectus in the eyes of readers. Any new venture requires time to establish effective working relationships, iron out difficulties, and learn from initial mistakes. *PM* was no exception. Some staff quit; some were let go. There was confusion with staff working at cross purposes. Ingersoll proposed many suggestions on how to improve the writing and focus of stories and editorials. He began sending memos to his staff, citing what he thought was wrong with the paper: not enough news or variety of news, articles too lengthy, not enough humor, and the fact that some of the news was stale by the time readers received their newspapers. "PM screams too loud and too often" was one comment regarding the crusading. Ingersoll called his staff "journalists of grief" when readers commented the paper was too negative and lacking in humor. On the positive side, *PM* was praised for its intelligence, independence, social consciousness, consumer interest, and inventiveness.[23] Seven months after its first issue, people were still talking about *PM,* even arguing about the paper. In another memorandum to staff, Ingersoll himself said, "It stinks, it's wonderful, it doesn't know what it's doing, it's not worth five cents, it's the only paper with the nerve to tell the truth . . ."[24]

An innovative, at the time, means of raising revenue was the sale of subscriptions. But because of prepublication hype and the high demand for the paper's first issue, and with readers overwhelming the delivery trucks and newsstands, *PM*'s papers could not be delivered to the subscribing customers. Papers were even stolen from *PM*'s trucks before subscribers' copies could be set aside. In addition, about 100,000 subscriber cards were somehow lost. The result was a loss of subscribers, and thus, revenue.

The paper sold for 5 cents, much more than the other dailies priced at 2 or 3 cents. Yet, the 370,000 copies of its first issue on June 18, 1940, quickly sold out, for as much as 50 cents, the demand was so great. Curiosity continued to fuel sellouts for the first few days but the enthusiasm would not last. After the initial sellout, circulation dropped to a low in August 1940 of 58,000 copies and then rose to an average of 100,000, which was much less than the required 200,000 to 250,000 to break even. Circulation continued to rise and fall over the eight years *PM* was in publication, rarely meeting the requirement to break even. To survive, *PM* would have to appeal to enough readers. Daily printing capacity of at most 300,000 copies was less than the larger metropolitan papers could produce and top printing press speed of only 40,000 copies per hour meant *PM* could not blanket the city with a late edition. In his interviews with Paul Milkman, Rae argued that *PM* did not offer enough to a mass audience particularly in a city already supporting nine daily papers. "I don't think women wanted a paper without advertising; our 'Best Buys' [section] didn't satisfy."[25]

Within weeks of the first edition, various groups boycotted it, spread malicious rumors about it, and sabotaged it on the newsstands. Newsstand sellers were uncooperative or worse, sometimes hiding copies and not displaying them. Ingersoll noted the right wing of the Catholic Church in the first month of publication boycotted *PM* and threw mud at their trucks. Opposing factions attacked the paper: the Fascists thought *PM* unfair to General Franco, Communists viewed *PM* as a Fascist plot, and the anti-labor movement called it Communist. In fact, *PM* was strongly pro-labor and anti-Fascist. In his December 21, 1940, memo to staff, Ingersoll even claimed Hitler "took a shot on the short wave now and then." While surviving these attacks, *PM* reached only half the circulation required to be financially viable.

PM's appeal among the general public was far from universal. A study of ninety-eight readers personally interviewed by C. E. Hooper, Inc. in September 1940 found the more favorable audience was by and large liberal and supported Roosevelt's New Deal; critics thought the paper did not live up to its initial ideals as it was too biased in its editorials and policies and lacked impartiality. Not everyone liked the emphasis on pictures that were so dear to Ingersoll. New Yorkers favored the sports, radio, and shopping sections while out-of-towners preferred foreign news, food news, and the photos.[26]

Several times in the first year, *PM* came close to going out of business.

On its first anniversary *PM* was losing $20,000 a week.[27] Rae remembered: "*PM* launched on June 18, 1940, and by September, Ingersoll had run out of money and the paper was bankrupt. About a third of that money was spent on promotion and publicity of the paper before it ever hit the streets. Marshall Field III, grandson of the founder of the great store in Chicago and one of the original stockholders, offered to buy the shares from the other investors at a fraction of their original investment (20 cents on the dollar) and assumed the entire financial responsibility for the paper." It should be noted that in 1943, Field was one of the richest men in America with a fortune of at least $168 million and an annual income of around $2 million.[28] Ingersoll knew by August 1940 that he had inadequate resources to continue; if he had not obtained financing to meet the payroll, there would have been no *PM*.

As noted previously, other publications found *PM*'s policy of taking no advertising a threat to their own business. At a time when most New York publications were conservative, they also disliked *PM*'s liberal philosophical stance. None did anything to assist the struggling paper, and some entities tried to thwart their success.

One example of this opposition was the refusal by the Associated Press to sell their wire service to *PM* as Rae recounted, "A side note about the Associated Press (AP): They operated as a monopoly, selling their service, the best wire service in the world, exclusively to certain papers. Hearst papers had their own wire service, the International News Service. The other main wire service was United Press, largely owned and financed by Scripps-Howard; they would sell their service to anyone. When *PM* started, United Press was the only service we could buy, leaving us at a disadvantage. No one had tried to break the Associated Press stranglehold until we presented the problem to Marshall Field who had started his *Chicago Sun* by this time. Field had his lawyers file suit against AP, accusing them of being a monopoly and denying their service to all but a select few." AP, the largest news-gathering agency in the nation then, was essentially discouraging competition among newspapers. Field's case was filed with the attorney general as a violation of the Sherman Antitrust Act of 1890 regulating restraint of trade. Eventually heard by the US Supreme Court, they decided the issue against the Associated Press in June 1945.[29]

Ingersoll also created some difficulties for *PM.* Rae explained how Ingersoll made it difficult for him to do his job: "Generally our reporters worked in the daytime with copy ready in the afternoon. I usually arrived between 1:00 and 2:00 in the afternoon. Dash came to work later in the afternoon around 3:00 or 4:00 and would go over the copy after it came from the copy desk; then it would go to the composing room to be set in type. Ralph would take the carbons home at 5:00 pm, returning for staff meetings around 9:00 pm with his 'corrected' carbons. By then the original edited copy was in type. Imagine trying to apply Ralph's corrections to the galley proofs, which already had been edited by copy readers and Dash Hammett—it would drive you nuts." Weimer recounted this nerve-wracking and expensive process to Tom Kirwan: "We were running up a hell of a bill with me trying to re-edit half the proofs . . . or giving it to the copy desk to do. It was a mess. And I argued with the composing room over whether they were my alterations or the proofreader's corrections. Every time a correction was made in the galley, they'd save the slugs they took out and, at the end of the day, we'd be charged for those corrections. I found out they were cheating us by taking all the typo corrections, too."[30]

17 *PM*'s Innovations

Almost everyone who has written about *PM* from the time of its inception to the present day, agrees that it was innovative journalism. More controversial are the opinions as to why this experiment ultimately failed. Rae reflected on *PM*'s impact. "I dare say no other paper had had such a thorough postmortem and burial as has *PM*. While this extraordinary pioneer, precedent-setting publication warranted this attention, I believe it deserved a more objective dissection rather than the prejudices and biases expressed in many of the articles about it. That is not to say Ingersoll's ideas were not excellent and nothing revolutionized the press of America like *PM* did. In talks given in my later years, I labeled my talk 'A Successful Failure,' stressing how *PM* revolutionized the form and content of the modern newspaper. *PM* failed after eight years but its successes mark every column of newspapers today, changed the whole method of reporting as well as the use of photographs, and generally made a profound impact on the American newspaper industry. Many of our innovations made us unpopular. Not because we were wrong, but because the public and the press were not ready to recognize some of the realities of the twentieth century. Our experimental ideas and innovations, shocking [at the time] to some of the skeptics, have now been adopted as everyday features in the modern newspaper. Newspapers now cover the news beats we created almost a half century ago. Perhaps it was Ingersoll's experience entirely with magazines where he established many innovations, made progressive changes in the methods and mechanics of publishing that led him to use these developments adopted by magazines for his ground-breaking daily newspaper. *PM* left its mark in journalism like nothing else—at least until my friend, Al Neuharth, put his *USA Today* on the market.

"Printing methods and *PM*'s format departed radically from the so-called standard press. One of the more controversial innovations was that *PM* would carry no paid advertising. It had long been the dream of many editors and reporters to work on a newspaper without advertising [in order to avoid being unduly influenced by the advertising entities.] Ingersoll's prospectus called for no paid advertising. In this radical move, he was encouraged by Nelson Poynter, publisher of the *St. Petersburg Times*. This sent a ripple of criticism through the metropolitan press—perhaps because they thought it might actually succeed.

"In format, the most noticeable idea was the compartmentalization of a daily paper. It wasn't difficult for a newspaper to begin to departmentalize its pages. Today we have sections that carry national news, local news, sports, entertainment, etc. An innovation we pioneered, now in common practice among newspapers and magazines today, was printing a table of radio stations and their programs in New York City. After the war when television came into being, we printed television schedules as well. I think *PM* introduced the coverage of health before any other newspaper did. In addition, we covered entertainment in New York such as music and movies and books, including reviews.

"Another drastic change *PM* made was in printing itself. Everyone complained about the carbon ink used on newspapers—[because] the ink came off on your hands and sometimes your clothes. We initially used a new kind of ink (Velox) that came in chunks. Special presses used steam heat on the plates to liquefy the ink; as the paper came across the rollers, it would solidify again so it didn't rub off. But when the United States entered the war, we no longer could get the ingredients and had to switch back to the common kind of ink everyone else used. We also pioneered wider columns and larger type; however, when we started taking advertising, we had to return to the standard narrow columns with nine-point type instead of ten-point. All for better readership, these techniques, revolutionary to the American press [at the time], brought concern to our immediate competitors, but set the pattern for change in succeeding years [in the newspaper business].

"We made a great impact with our maps particularly during the war. We mapped the battles of World War II from beginning to end: where they fought in Europe, where they fought in the Pacific, so people understood where ships, armies, and fighting occurred. To do this we had two full-time mapmakers on staff. It is interesting that the *New York Times* had never carried any kind of art on the front page, but after seeing our maps, they began to carry a war map on page one, too. Shortly, the Associated Press began to produce war maps they sent to all their clients.

"[We were also] years ahead of our time in handling of consumer news, called 'News for Living.' Our consumer news features included our crusades or campaigns to expose dishonesty and racketeering at the expense of the consumer. One example was the selling of 'watered meat.' We sent reporters to dozens of markets to buy meat samples which we then had analyzed at a laboratory. Sometimes 50 percent of the samples were soaked with brine, exceeding the legal limit for brine preservative. Other exposures were the sale of sick poultry and installment sales practices, a racket in selling used cars. *PM* was very much in support of trade unions and strongly advocated collective bargaining. *PM* was one of the leaders, if not the leader, in New York against racial intolerance, campaigning hard to change New York State's laws regarding the advertising of apartments that had been discriminatory; *PM* lobbied to prohibit the use of words like *White* and *Christian* in apartment rental ads. I think we were the only paper that strongly supported the establishment of the first biracial hospital in New York. Another injustice we addressed was hiring African American domestics off the street and paying them substandard wages. We campaigned for discount stores to be able to cut prices. We exposed companies like Standard Oil for selling oil to the Nazis. *PM* never straddled the fence. Instead of being credited with doing the city consumers a service, we were unfavorably criticized for the 'sick chicken' stories. We had a lawyer full-time in our office to check our stories because we hit very hard, we named markets, gave addresses [and exposed wrongdoers]. I think many other newspapers were afraid to run such exposés for two reasons: One was for libel but the other was because merchants would pull their advertising. [In the first six months alone, *PM* crusaded against sixty-seven injustices.[31]] Where *PM* was a pioneer, today all newspapers routinely cover labor, education, the press; we were more than a decade ahead in our handling of minority news and calling for someone to address their problems. While *PM* never hesitated to go on a crusade to expose and ferret out dishonesty, I think it supported our creed that we searched for the truth.

"But don't get the idea that is all we did, we published lots of stories that were amusing, entertaining, and informative to readers. One marvelous story we did was about the Roosevelts' neighbors and people who lived around their home up the Hudson River at Hyde Park. We sent a photographer and reporter up to interview and photograph them—where and how they lived, what they did and thought. They were just common simple people like the rest of us. One was the caretaker who took care of the Roosevelt estate when he was not in residence. Then there was a man living on a small farm adjacent to Hyde Park. Another individual lived in a little house with a wood-burning stove in his living room right next to this millionaire Roosevelt family; he was known to the Roosevelts as Uncle Ben. Before he was president, Roosevelt had met a sailor that he later hired as his woodsman. The story of about six pages gave the general public a picture of what the Roosevelt estate was like."

A reciprocal relationship existed between *PM* and the Roosevelts. The newspaper wholeheartedly supported Roosevelt's New Deal and liberal policies. Eleanor and Franklin Roosevelt both read and promoted *PM*—FDR sent a congratulatory letter directly to Ralph Ingersoll, and Eleanor praised *PM* in her nationally syndicated column, "My Day." "We were one of the few, if only, newspaper that seemed to support [Roosevelt] in all of his ideas and proposals," Rae recalled. "Roosevelt ran into much opposition with some of his proposals during the early days of the depression. When Germany and Russia were gobbling up small countries and dividing them up between them, *PM* was almost the lone voice among the press advocating the United States prepare for war. Roosevelt was pretty helpless to get anything started in that regard, but was grateful, I think, for the voice he got from us. Because of that close relationship between *PM* and Roosevelt, he was available to us anytime we wanted to call him for inside information or assistance. In December 1941, probably with the help of Roosevelt, Ingersoll traveled to Russia to interview Stalin. I believe it was the first time Stalin had ever granted an interview to a reporter from the West."

18 The War Years

Unlike many Americans at the time, *PM* was internationalist not isolationist. "Those turbulent times were marked by a strong wave of isolationism in the land," Rae said, "led by the powerful *Chicago Tribune* in the Middle West, the *Times Herald* in Washington, and the *New York Daily News.* They saw little danger for America in what was going on abroad, and many other newspapers supported the idea or remained silent. *PM*, by contrast, perceived a close relationship of America to what was going on overseas. *PM* took a strong position of internationalism, warning all who would read and listen that we needed to prepare for the day when we would be forced to become involved. Early in my career [at *PM*] we advocated going to war against Hitler but found little support for such a position.

"In 1941, *PM* was the voice in the wilderness advocating joining the war and then the draft started in 1942. Ralph Ingersoll, who was then about forty-two years old, got his draft notice. He argued that newspaper editors should be exempt as necessary to the war effort and filed suit. The case was eventually decided in his favor, but by then, as a matter of principle having advocated the United States go to war, Ralph enlisted. Ingersoll distinguished himself throughout his tour of duty. Finally attached to Eisenhower's staff in England, Ralph was the one who designed the diversion for the invasion of France . . . including coming up with the idea of using phony boats and other decoys to confuse the Germans about the site of the D-Day landing. [Desirous of serving his county, Rae applied to both the Army and Navy but was rejected due to an 'inability to meet the physical requirements,' most likely in reference to his damaged right arm and hand.] "I wanted to serve, but they said I couldn't shoot. Imagine that, I hunted all the time, even after my broken arm left my right arm damaged.[32]

"Actually, Ingersoll was editor of *PM* less than three years. When George Lyon left to join the Office of War Information, John Lewis moved up to editor and I became managing editor. We were more comfortable after Ralph was in the army and the paper was more standardized."[33] Ralph could be insistent on getting his own way, often interfering in the operation of the paper. Rae told one story of how the staff got around Ingersoll's insistence on running a page two summary of all the best big news stories: "We went along with this for quite a long time until a couple of us decided it was a waste of space and suggested to Ralph that we drop it. 'No,' he said, 'that is one of the best things in the paper.' He simply wasn't going to drop that news summary. So one day we had somebody set it in French and ran it. The next night at our staff meeting we asked Ralph if he was still convinced the summary was a good idea. When he replied, 'Yes,' we showed it to him and he acknowledged he had not been reading it himself. Then we got to drop it!"

Despite the innovations and radical policies, *PM* never became self-supporting. Circulation fluctuated but never consistently reached the 200,000 to 250,000 mark required to break even. Before Ingersoll enlisted in the Army, he tried to correct *PM*'s deficiencies, writing innumerable memoranda in which he reiterated his initial goals or seemed to blame the staff for the paper's shortcomings. Ingersoll tried to hire writers whose literary style was the kind he thought appropriate for a newspaper, writing with these characteristics: well-understood, everyday words; short sentences without unnecessary words; a feeling for the dramatic; and able to connect with people.[34]

A reading through innumerable memoranda Ingersoll sent to his staff during *PM*'s early years makes it clear he was a visionary and a dreamer but not a realist. At times, he came across as arrogant and self-righteous. He frequently requoted or resent his original ideas, set out in his prospectus, for staff to reread. He criticized his staff, laying much of the blame for *PM*'s poor circulation on them, chastising staff for their poor writing skills, and suggesting shorter sentences, simpler words, and less description. Yet, when one reads his lengthy memos from 1940 to 1942, Ingersoll's own writing was anything but pithy and concise. It is no wonder that many staff were relieved when he enlisted in the Army and deployed to Europe.

New editor John Lewis continued the original liberal philosophy upon which *PM* had been founded, bemoaning an incoming Congress in his November 25, 1942, memo to the staff: "New Congress is going to try all kinds of monkey business to upset the social advances made during the last few years. We are going to have to do something . . . not only for our liberal cause but for *PM*. We are probably the most effective voice in the country on the side of liberalism."[35]

Lewis described Weimer's new duties as: laying out each day's paper including allotment of space for each department, feature, and picture; consulting with all department editors to determine which stories would be features and whether they would be told in words or pictures; making sure all the news was covered and that all stories conformed to the paper's policies. Basically, Rae was responsible for the production of the paper. His direct supervision of the entire editorial staff entailed checking and approving all expense accounts, purchasing stories/pictures, supervising hiring/firing of staff, plus office management. To carry out these duties, Lewis noted, required an individual willing to work long hours, well-versed in libel laws, knowledgeable in wartime censorship regulations, and capable of directing the entire newspaper operation in his absence.[36]

Volta Torrey, who spent a few unforgettable years with *PM* before editing *Popular Science* and *Technology Review*, said of Rae's professional style: "Staff meetings went on for hours but Rae rarely said much and quietly ignored silly notions and foolhardy decisions. He had the rare knack of making a news story printable without offending whoever had written it. The paper could not have survived as long as it did without Rae's steady hand on the steering wheel."[37]

An "inveterate prankster" and one who tolerated outrageous practical jokes were two descriptions of the high-spirited Rae. Tension and stress from newspaper deadlines were often relieved by various stunts. Rae described such pranks to Myra MacPherson.[38] "Special nights after working late on a story, like the Roosevelt campaign, some of us would go up on the roof and dump a bucket of water down on the copydesk and everyone below." Rae himself was the victim of this when staff climbed up to the skylight and dumped water all over his copydesk. But he was also the perpetrator of a prank when Ralph Ingersoll was leaving for Russia to cover the war as Rae recounted: "When Ralph went out the front door to get in his car, we began dropping lighted firecrackers down around him from the second floor to get him toughened up for the war front!" Rae, in a phone interview with Paul Milkman, author of *PM: A New Deal in Journalism,* told about a prank he and the city editor pulled on John Lewis, involving breaking into Lewis's apartment to leave a live rabbit and a dozen baby chicks for Easter. Apprehended by a policeman, the two were able to convince the policeman that Lewis really wanted the birds.[39] A favorite pastime with the staff was a regular poker game organized by Rae. "It surprised no one that he frequently won."[40] When staff encountered high temperatures at night, John A. Sullivan recounted to Milkman that Rae would allow staff to strip to their underwear to avoid their clothing becoming soaked with sweat.[41]

During the time *PM* took no advertising, the paper finished with a profit only one year, 1945, due in large part to a delivery strike against *PM*'s competitors. *PM* not only benefited from the strike but actually made a profit of $40,000 that year. Favorable to the unions, *PM* had signed a contract with the union representing those who delivered the papers and saw circulation increase by around 300,000 additional papers daily during the seventeen-day strike. Employees reaped the rewards when, at the end of 1945, the $40,000 profit was apportioned among them.[42]

19 A Dream of a Family

During their marriage, Rae's and Arletta's careers took different paths as they each worked in separate cities and drifted apart. Rae explained, "Arletta and I divorced in early 1942. I learned several years later that while she was working in Chicago, she contracted some kind of blood disease, which doctors thought she got in the composing room where she supervised the makeup of her pages. This rare blood disease so baffled the doctors in Chicago that they flew in a doctor from Sweden and spent several thousand dollars trying to treat her. She died there not too many months after she contracted the disease at age forty-five."

Although Rae had met his future wife, Ruth Meister, in Akron, circumstances intervened in their courtship with Rae moving several times and Ruth returning to Oklahoma City, where she worked for the Oklahoma Publishing Company from October 1938 until November 1942. Rae briefly described what happened next in their romance. "During the time after I left Akron, went to Buffalo, then to Cleveland, and finally to New York City, Ruth and I had kept in touch by letter, telegraph, and telephone. Still in the midst of the war, I took a vacation in June 1942 to visit Ruth in Oklahoma City. We decided to get married." Rae and Ruth announced their engagement during a small breakfast at her home in Oklahoma City. Adorning each place and printed on copy paper was the following: "From Eastern-Coastal Front—One personal bodyguard needed for the duration somewhere in New York beginning sometime in early November, 1942. By: Rae O Weimer, commanding general. Mid-Western Theater—Combat and non-combat duties accepted as of Oct. 17, 1942. By Ruth Meister, non-technical sergeant. Approved by: Dan Cupid, commandant of all armed forces."

"Ruth came to New York, and we were married November 5, 1942," Rae continued. "Guests were John and Carol Lewis; Edith Gaylord, daughter of the owner of the Oklahoma papers, who was then working for the

Associated Press in New York; and another society editor from Oklahoma and her husband. After the ceremony, we 'splurged' that day and instead of using the subway as I normally would, we went by taxicab to the Granada Hotel where we would be residing for a few months." Ruth had to settle for a 5-cent ride on the Staten Island Ferry for a honeymoon.[43]

Before the marriage, Rae had been living at the Granada Hotel in New York City, an establishment that was partly residential and also housed various offices and businesses. After their marriage the newlyweds maintained these accommodations for a few months. Rae explained the benefits of this arrangement: "We had a kind of two-room suite with a living room, a bedroom, a bath, and a small kitchenette. With the hours I was working, I usually didn't get up until the middle of the morning, and what would be my breakfast was Ruth's lunch. Often, we ate in the hotel dining room. Around dinnertime I'd come back and eat with Ruth." Ruth related that, "I didn't even have to make the beds."[44] Next, they rented a furnished apartment in Jackson Heights from one of *PM*'s photographers, which afforded more convenient public transportation for Rae.

Because Rae worked at night and into the early morning hours, he and Ruth could spend their afternoons enjoying the sights of New York. Rae described his feelings about living in New York: "Ruth and I both thoroughly enjoyed living in New York, particularly going to the theater. We'd arrive at the theater about thirty minutes before curtain time and ask for balcony tickets, the least expensive because in some theaters the seats are so far away you can hardly see the stage. Since few people in these less expensive seats cancelled, no tickets would be available so close to curtain time, but theaters often had cancellations for the more expensive seats in the main theater downstairs. If we were lucky, we'd get those better seats for the price of a balcony seat. Since the theaters were so close together, if we couldn't get a better ticket at one, we could walk next door and try the same thing again. Sometimes we would go to two or three theaters before we got in, but we were seeing some of the best Broadway shows for only a few dollars. Other pursuits we enjoyed were the fights, follies, and circus in Madison Square Garden. A favorite excursion was to catch the nickel ferry to Staten Island where we might enjoy a stroll or have dinner before returning to the Bowery for another nickel. In the summer, Ruth and I would escape the city heat for fresh air on a steamer from lower Manhattan up the Hudson River to Bear Mountain State Park. The park afforded shaded picnic groves along the lake or river. Strolling through the park there or just lounging on cool grass was refreshing.[45] Visiting John and Carol Lewis was another favorite pastime."

Ruth and Rae's dream of starting a family came true in 1943 when they learned they would become parents the following spring. Ruth made the announcement to her friends and previous newspaper colleagues with the following, "'Confidential Release' for publication 'after late March': Come spring, Rae and I have a priority application signed and approved by Dr. Stork. This human dynamo we hope will have red, curly hair and blue eyes and follow a routine that won't interfere too much with a night-working newspaperman's schedule." On schedule, their son, Rae O. Weimer, II arrived April 1, 1944. *PM* even announced the birth of a potential future "copyboy" when Rae's son was born: "Yesterday Rae became the father of a boy . . . who weighed in at 7 pounds, 9 ounces. That's a little light for our purposes, but give him time and I guess he'll make it."[46] Named Rae O. Weimer, II after his father, the proud parents decided to call this bundle of joy "Bill" in homage to Rae's own nickname as a boy.

Rationing of consumer goods during World War II affected everyone; there was even black market trading. The war disrupted trade and the supply of food, gas, and household items. Such foodstuffs as sugar, coffee, meats, cheese, milk, and canned goods were all rationed. The government encouraged Americans to plant Victory Gardens to provide some of their own food.

"During the war we were sending so much food overseas that food was rationed nationally," Rae said. "We used different colored stamps to obtain provisions—red for meat and blue for canned goods. I think we fared better than most because my brother Doc was butchering his own meat on his farm and would send us his red stamps. When we got word of a butcher on Long Island, we used our red stamps to get a quarter of beef cut, packaged, and frozen. Ruth made friends with the local grocer in order to get milk as there was not enough for everyone. The grocer would put it under the counter so that strangers coming in would see no milk for sale, but regular customers could buy the milk the grocer stashed away for them." Although many goods were hard to come by during the war years, the new parents were resourceful, as Rae explained, "Much of our furniture was purchased through auction: Manhattan dealers would go out and buy an entire estate, bring it into their salesrooms and have auctions that were advertised in the paper daily.

"When Bill was about a year old, I slipped on a piece of paper on the subway steps one night coming home from the office. The next morning X-rays showed a leg fracture; I was given crutches but no cast. Not able to work for about a week, I enjoyed a great time with Bill playing around my bed beside me. Still on crutches, I secured a rather expensive means of transport back to the office—a limousine at $25 each way for a couple of weeks. At the time I hadn't realized that using crutches could cut off the blood supply in my arms and body giving me a severe case of pleurisy, which was quite painful. I returned to work when I felt better but had a relapse and was told to leave New York. We decided the warmest place was Palm Beach, but since it was still during the war, you couldn't get a train reservation as trains were reserved for troop movements. *PM* exerted some influence and I headed to Palm Beach where I would lay out on the beach and let the sun bake the poison out of me. I found it amazing how the sun helped me recover from pleurisy when medication had not. [Most likely it was the rest, relaxation, and absence of stress that healed Rae's lungs.] On my return to New York three weeks later, I stopped in Daytona Beach to visit Herb Davidson and his wife. He had been our national editor at *PM* and was instrumental in bringing me to Florida in 1949.

"I mentioned previously about the summer heat in New York during the war years when air-conditioning was rare because there was very little manufacturing of appliances. None of the apartments seemed to have it so people in New York tried to get outside the city, often to Long Island or up the Hudson River toward the mountains. In the summer of 1945, we bought a cottage up in the Ramapo Mountains of New Jersey at Cozy Lake after looking in other locations. I believe the price was $3,600. To get to the cottage we had to buy a car, so we bought a second-hand Ford Roadster for $300 that certainly wasn't worth any more than that. Ruth would drive back and forth and pick me up. It seemed like it rained most of that summer, but the cottage had two screened porches where Bill, who was fifteen or sixteen months old, could get outdoors to a degree and play on the porches. Between showers Ruth would put Bill in a wagon and go down to the little store for groceries. We sold the cottage sometime that fall after Ruth came back to New York."

The daughter Ruth prayed for to complete her family arrived March 14, 1946, at Doctor's Hospital, in the borough of Queens, New York, with her father's reddish-blond hair but hazel eyes. She was named Helen Ann Weimer out of respect for Ruth's only sister, Helen, who had already named her only child Ruth Carolyn Arbuckle. Each sister used their daughters' middle names, Ann and Carolyn.

Another example of Rae's creativity in solving problems was evident in the following vignette he recounted: "In anticipation of the arrival of our son, Bill, we moved to a larger apartment, then an even larger apartment when our daughter, Ann, arrived, all the while remaining in Jackson Heights. There were about eighty families in our building, which meant a lot of children. So, we organized our own nursery school in the basement, had it certified by the city, and hired a teacher. It was an ideal setup. Those were the days when we were fearful of polio, so we didn't take the kids out anywhere they might be exposed, which left walks outdoors or trips to [see John and Carol] Lewis." *PM,* with its emphasis on pictures, posted a two-page spread about the new cooperative nursery school with only a quarter of the space devoted to copy and the rest of the piece featuring photos of the children.[47]

20 *PM* Ceases Publication

Discharged from the Army in July 1945, Ingersoll did not immediately return to *PM*. During the six months before he did return, he married then retired to his Connecticut home to write his war memoirs.[48] As Rae told it, "By the time Ingersoll returned from the war, we had revamped our setup, and I don't think Ralph felt comfortable with the way we were doing things." Still wanting to be in total control, Ingersoll had sought major staff changes after penning a lengthy discourse on what was wrong with the paper—that it was "more of a liberal crusading sheet than a newspaper"—exactly the kind of paper his prospectus had envisioned.[49] Paul Milkman posits that Ingersoll thought his newspaper had been commandeered by a Lewis-Weimer organization.[50]

At the end of the war, *PM* had been doing relatively well financially, but with both a change in the political tone of the new administration and inflation, a crisis loomed. Taking advertising seemed the only way to save the struggling paper; Weimer and Lewis agreed but Ingersoll did not. In October 1946, Ingersoll penned a letter to Marshall Field, published in the November 5, 1946, issue of *PM*, lamenting that increasing costs had put *PM* in the red again and that still higher costs seemed inevitable. Although understanding the need to now take advertising, Ingersoll could not compromise his principle that there should be at least one newspaper in America supported solely by readers. With that, Ingersoll resigned from *PM*. Rae reflected on Ingersoll's decision: "The reason he gave for departing was that he opposed Marshall Field's decision to start taking advertising. And that may have had some bearing on it, but I think it was used more as an excuse than anything else." Rae told Paul Milkman that he believed the decision to take advertising gave Ingersoll an excuse to resign from a newspaper he no longer controlled and one that had not lived up to his unrealistic dreams. Weimer and Lewis were "delighted to see him go."[51] *PM* decided to accept advertising once Ingersoll left as Rae further recounted. "Eventually, we did take advertising, and the first year we made a profit of $100,000. Marshall Field gave half of that to our staff, divided equally from the editors down to the copyboys.

"In the fall of 1947, John Lewis and I discussed *PM*'s prospects and concluded it was not a going concern the way it was then constituted, being subsidized by Marshall Field. We shared our concerns with Field, suggesting the only hope was to change the format, maybe go to a national daily. (It is interesting that while he turned down the idea, not wanting to try something new, the second greatest innovation in journalism of the twentieth century, after *PM*, was *USA Today*, a daily paper using many of the innovations *PM* pioneered.) Field's *Chicago Sun* was doing well, and he asked us if we would stay on that year until he could sell *PM*, which wasn't a very salable property. *PM* died in June 1948, and no publication has ever been given such a thorough postmortem and burial as has been accorded to this precedent-setting publication. Some verification of the widespread press comment about this newspaper I found in a thesis written in 1948 at New York University, which carried a bibliography on *PM* of more than twelve pages."

Several newspaper articles in March 1948 announced the pending sale of *PM* to publisher Clinton D. McKinnon dependent on acceptance by the *PM* chapter of the Newspaper Guild of New York. Employees received notices in their mailboxes stating, "To all *PM* employees. You are hereby notified that your employment with *PM* will terminate at the close of business on Friday, March 26, 1948."[52] The existing Guild contract included severance pay for anyone resigning or leaving *PM*, but McKinnon sought to eliminate that clause, change the sick leave policy, and have unrestricted hiring and firing rights. In the end, the Newspaper Guild rejected McKinnon's demands and he withdrew his offer to purchase the moribund paper.

By April 1948, Marshall Field III made the decision to sell a controlling interest in *PM* to Joseph Barnes, editor of the *New York Herald Tribune*, and Bartley Crumb, a liberal San Francisco attorney who represented the underdog and defended targets of the House Un-American Activities Committee. Field had reportedly lost anywhere from $4 to $10 million on *PM* and was then more interested in his fledgling *Chicago Sun*.

Max Lerner penned a "Farewell and Hail" in the April 29, 1948, *PM* issue announcing the agreement of sale:

> Part of the test of a paper's vigor is the enemies it makes. There were many, I am sure, who rejoiced when they heard that *PM* might fold. . . . In a democracy there is an important function for searching and outspoken criticism, and that is what *PM* has done . . . in subjecting the crasser forms of power and injustice to a raking fire. But it has also fought affirmatively for the things that decent Americans believe in. Although many papers have had a larger body of readers, no paper has ever had readers so devoted. No paper, I think it is fair to say, has ever entered the lives of its readers as deeply and been as fiercely debated. The world of American newspapers is different and better because of the fact of *PM*'s existence.

In the words of I. F. Stone, *PM* was a "gallant defeat, which is more glorious than a victory because it was something original, courageous, and different."[53] Just after *PM*'s last issue on June 22, 1948, Barnes's and Crumb's first edition of the renamed *New York Star* hit newsstands on June 23, 1948. This reincarnation of *PM* also folded seven months later on January 28, 1949, ending what had been a revolutionary experiment in journalism that would nevertheless influence the field of journalism for years to come.

Throughout its few years of publishing, *PM* faced repeated financial and operational crises too great to ultimately overcome. Opposed by other New York newspapers, *PM* encountered difficulty even getting its maiden issue on the newsstands. It took a lawsuit to obtain rights to purchase all wire services. Circulation rose and fell but rarely reached a level enabling *PM* to make a profit, much less break even. Undoubtedly there were many reasons given for *PM*'s dissolution.

Rae gave his own assessment of *PM*'s demise: "As I looked back after *PM* folded and analyzed his [Ingersoll's] prospectus, I don't believe any group of editors and reporters could have put out the kind of publication he perceived for his new kind of newspaper. My own evaluation of why we ceased publication was that *PM*'s pioneering efforts were ahead of their time. If any one thing caused *PM*'s failure, I think it was twenty-five years ahead of its time. For me, it continued to operate as a subsidized newspaper, and I don't believe any newspaper should so exist in the public interest. Ingersoll had no idea of the difficulties he would have implementing all of his ideas in a daily publication when he had been accustomed to weekly publications. Yet, I believe people were not ready to endorse or support efforts on their behalf in the consumer field. Today there are publications devoted entirely to consumer news and every newspaper prints consumer news daily. Perhaps we didn't reach the right audience—those we tried to help were not the people who bought the paper. We didn't fulfill Ingersoll's dream, but I have never been convinced that anybody could have done all the things he envisioned for the paper. None of the staff had ever worked on such a paper under such an aegis as was set for *PM*. Ingersoll himself didn't know how it could be done; he just dreamed that such a publication was possible.

"In 1948, I thought *PM* had failed. Years later, as I looked back, I viewed it differently as *PM* took its place in journalism history. I reminisced about those eight years in which *PM* flourished, sagged, and struggled for a place in the highly competitive market of eleven daily newspapers. As editors and writers we failed in fulfilling some of our lofty goals, but that did not mark career failures for any of us. History records that *PM* as an entity was not a complete failure. I labeled some of my talks about *PM* in later years 'A Successful Failure,' referring to its profound influence on the newspaper industry."

David Margolick in his 1999 feature for *Vanity Fair* aptly summed up *PM:* "Yet *PM* lives on in every American newspaper. With larger and blacker type, bigger and better pictures, wider margins, cleaner layout, and great use of color, it was 'reader-friendly' long before the term was coined. *PM* was the first paper to have radio and movie listings and to cover consumer affairs, labor, and the press itself."[54]

Marshall Field wanted Rae to tell *PM*'s story. "I had been in Florida about two years when I received a letter from Marshall Field asking me if I would be willing to talk with him in Chicago about *PM*. I thought if I went to see him maybe I could get some money from him as a grant or something for the School [of Journalism]. When I met with Marshall in Chicago, he said he wanted me to take a year off from my job in Florida to write the history of *PM*. Of course, he would pay me my regular salary and whatever expenses I needed to gather information from former staff at *PM,* but it would be necessary to go back to New York to do most of it. As I had only been at the university a couple of years, I didn't feel I could spare the time at that stage, so I had to tell him 'No.' And, he had to tell me 'No' with regard to any grant or money for the school. So, that ended there. I don't believe anybody has really ever told the full story of *PM* although there have been hundreds of articles written about *PM.* As late as 1987, some of the magazines were still writing about *PM.*" This incident was related by Rae Weimer in 1988. In fact, at least one comprehensive history of *PM* was written by Paul Milkman (*PM: A New Deal in Journalism 1940–1948*) and published in 2016. Milkman was able to interview Weimer by phone in 1994. In later years, Rae gave several talks to various organizations in Gainesville, Florida, on *PM*'s impact on journalism.

21 Yet Another Move

The demise of *PM* created a challenging period for all of *PM*'s employees. Rae described how he coped. "Of course, the new owners wanted a clean sweep of personnel, particularly the editors, so we were all cut loose. For some time, Ruth and I had been discussing, knowing that *PM* was not viable, that New York would be a poor place to raise and school our children. Believing that none of the other papers in town wanted any of us, I did not apply for a job with any of them, although I did make a number of inquiries with other businesses including a soap company in Boston. The soap company offered me a job at $25,000 a year primarily to write speeches. Ruth and I were not very enthusiastic about moving from one metropolitan city to another, plus I had no experience writing speeches."

Another job Rae applied for was with a general news bureau in Schenectady, New York. He sought a change from his twenty years of mastering every newspaper job from cub to managing editor and thought he could do a "bang-up job" in public relations. His application letter referred to the ill-fated purchase of the daily paper in North Platte, "in six months we went broke, and I have been chasing wrong fonts ever since." As word of *PM*'s dissolution spread, Rae was contacted by the managing editor of the *Cincinnati Post* who wanted "to make a bid" for him, and he received a wire from Indianapolis where he had previously worked "asking for a chance at [his] services." Rae took pride in these offers he felt were based on the reputation he had established for himself in the newspaper business over many years.

Rae also applied to *Better Homes and Gardens* and asked John Lewis to write him a recommendation. In his letter to the editor, Lewis wrote of Rae:

> One of his outstanding qualifications for any job is his ability to fit into an organization and work effectively with others . . . with as little

friction and with as much efficiency as any man I have ever known. Not a "yes" man . . . for he is forthright and outspoken—he gets along by his frankness, his ability, his willingness to carry more than a fair share of the load, and by a native knack of getting along with folks. He is able to transmit ideas to those who work for him without using a bludgeon, getting top-quality work from inexperienced help. At heart, Weimer is an editor—one of those rare creative individuals who finds his expression and pleasure, not by writing under his own name, but by direction and working with other writers to get into print a product that is better than either of them could produce alone. He can write better than passably himself, but he prefers the role of editor and he is tops at it. Weimer is an excellent editor, a fine printing craftsman, and a warm, personable human. He is interested in good stories, in people and how they live. He doesn't carry a political banner for anyone or any party. He's sort of a normal mid-country American, goes to church occasionally, to the movies more often, and enjoys living. He is honest, energetic, youthful, and is backed up at home by a swell, young family. He gives more to both his work and his family life than most, and I would back him to lick any job put before him.[55]

Rae took none of these jobs, explaining, "At the same time, Doc had been writing me to come join his advertising and public relations agency, the Weimer Organization, in Columbus, Ohio. With that offer, we packed up and left New York behind. Unable to find an apartment, we moved into a two-story, 125-year-old house on Doc's farm. My parents also lived on the farm in a third home.

"The farm of about 400 acres was eight miles east of Columbus and two miles from a little town—Gahanna—of maybe 500 residents, about the size of Mason City. We enjoyed the freedom of outdoors and a smaller community living outside both Gahanna and Columbus. Still, I needed a car to drive to work daily. Because of Doc's friendship with the local Chevrolet dealer, he sold us two cars. Ours was a red Chevrolet, the car I had when we came to Florida. We were able to purchase the car using my separation pay of $1,250 that Field paid all the Newspaper Guild Members when *PM* folded.

"Winter 1949 was an unfortunate one. I had a severe case of bursitis in my right shoulder requiring surgery to remove the calcium from the bursa—one of the most painful ailments I ever had. The operation involved throwing the shoulder out of place and digging out the calcium that had collected in the bursa. (I had bursitis again in the other shoulder about two years after the move to Florida, returning to Ohio where the same doctor performed the identical operation on my other shoulder.) A month or two after the bursitis that winter, both my children caught the mumps. I had never had the disease even though I had slept in the same bed with Doc when he had the mumps as a child. Without any immunity, I was quite ill.

"Life on the farm in Columbus was great primarily for the freedom it afforded Bill and Ann. In New York, when we took the kids out for a walk, Ruth had to have a harness on Bill as she pushed Ann's baby buggy. The harness was necessary to keep small youngsters from darting out into traffic. On the farm they were free to play outdoors wherever they wanted. My dad practically took over Bill, taking him everywhere he went. Bill loved to sit up on the tractor with my dad. So fond of the farm was Bill, that when it was time to move to Florida, Bill decided he wasn't coming—he was going to stay on the farm! We also had the pleasure of my parents' company as well as that of Doc and his family."

In the next chapter of Rae's life, the visions would be his, but they would be realistic and practical. The control would be his, but he would delegate to others and learn from their expertise. Confidence in his own abilities engendered by his vast experiences and lessons learned from others would enable him to succeed and leave a lasting legacy.

David F. Weimer, Rae's paternal grandfather.

Mary Kryder Weimer, Rae's paternal grandmother.

Weimer home, Mason City, Nebraska.

Rae Weimer's college photo.

Ruth Meister (*center front*) college photo.

Ruth Meister (*left*) interviews Eleanor Roosevelt (*right*).

Left to right, Rae Weimer, Alexander Uhl, John Lewis, and Ralph Ingersoll at *PM* (*PM*/Steven Derry).

"Boss" Rae Weimer at *PM* (*PM*/John Albert).

Rae Weimer (*far right, seated*) in the newsroom of *PM*.

Rae and Ruth on their first international trip to Honduras, circa 1943.

Left to Right: Elmer J. Emig; John Paul Jones, Jr.; William L. Lowry; Rae O. Weimer, Director; Edward C. Hanna.

University of Florida School of Journalism's first faculty (*Communigator*).

Building K—University of Florida School of Journalism's first home (*Communigator*).

University of Florida School of Journalism's stadium home (*Communigator*).

Rae and Ruth, early years in Gainesville.

Journalism's first Hearst Award: (*left to right*) President Lyndon Johnson, Hugh Cunningham, Rae Weimer, University of Florida president J. Wayne Reitz (AP Photo/ William J. Smith).

College of Journalism and Communication's first three deans: (*left to right*) Rae Weimer, John Paul Jones, Ralph Lowenstein (*Communigator*).

Rae Weimer in front of Weimer Hall 1981 (*Communigator*).

Weimer family: (*left to right*) Rae, Ruth, Kitty (Rae's mother), Curtis (Rae's father), Ann, Lillian (Doc's wife).

The Weimer family's 1961 European tour.

Rae and Wilma Weimer.

Rae, Ann, Jim Solar (Ann's husband), and Wilma take the Napa Valley wine train.

The Weimers, 1990: (*standing*) Wilma, Rae, Ann, Bill, Eathel (Bill's wife); (*front*) Ryan and Hunter (grandsons).

Rae with one of his many awards, the Rotary Service Above Self Award, 1989.

PART IV

University of Florida

22 Florida Beckons

After working eight years for the most innovative newspaper endeavor in US history, Rae Weimer was the creative force in establishing one of the most innovative journalism programs in the nation. How Rae Weimer ended up at the University of Florida was not straightforward. He did not seek the position, but those familiar with his talents and like-minded newspapermen who appreciated his skills recommended him.

While working with his brother in Ohio, a golden career opportunity now presented itself. Rae recounted how this came about: "In the early spring of 1949, about the time I was recovering from the mumps, I got a call from Herbert Davidson, whose father owned the *Daytona Beach News-Journal.* When *PM* came on the scene, Herb was much intrigued by it and became the national editor for *PM;* later he returned to Florida to run his father's paper (probably the most liberal editor in Florida).[1] Herb wanted to know if I was interested in starting a School of Journalism at the University of Florida. That was a surprise! Herb told me Florida's daily newspapers had been agitating for upgrading journalism education at the university for some time, and they found a responsive person in President J. Hillis Miller. Miller had submitted the names of several PhD English teachers one after another to the editors and [the newspapermen] turned all of them down. They told Miller they wanted somebody who would create a School of Journalism that would produce reporters they could use, and they had no confidence in English professors being able to do the job. Miller told them, 'You guys go out and find somebody then; you don't like people that I get.' [At the time] journalism graduates knew nothing about working for newspapers. The professional newspapermen were frustrated with the university's previous applicants for the job—highly degreed individuals with master's and doctorate degrees. The newspaper associations in Florida wanted a newspaperman with experience, and it became their job to find an acceptable candidate."

Davidson, as head of the committee to find a suitable candidate, who knew Weimer when they both worked at *PM*, said, "I happen to know [Rae] didn't like public relations work worth a damn."[2] "Rae had excellent news judgment—he was a thoroughly trained newspaper technician. I was impressed with his sympathetic handling [of the young *PM* journalists]. He had some teaching instinct."[3]

"Herb Davidson told me the Daily Newspaper Association and the Weekly Association were going to meet in Gainesville in early spring and wanted me to come down for an interview," Rae remembered. "When I went to Gainesville for the interview, I was just barely back on my feet from the mumps. Taking a bus to Daytona Beach from the Jacksonville airport, I stayed with Herb and his wife. The next day we drove to Gainesville to meet with two other newspapermen, Bill Pepper as editor of the *Gainesville Sun* and Henry Wren of the *Tallahassee Democrat;* along with J. Hillis Miller, president of the University of Florida; Ralph Page, dean of the College of Arts and Sciences; Registrar Dick Johnson; and Harley Chandler, dean of academic affairs. That was the strangest interview I ever encountered. They had no idea what to ask me and I had no idea what to tell them because I had no experience in a School of Journalism, had never even taken a journalism class. They didn't speak my language and I didn't speak theirs. We basically exchanged pleasantries and talked generalities. Finally, Miller addressed the newspapermen, 'Is this the man you want?' and they said, 'Yes, this is the man we want.' With that, Miller indicated he would submit my name for approval."

Rae was also able to meet with the only three faculty members at that time, Elmer Emig, who was then chairman of the department; William Lowry; and John Paul Jones, who had just come down from Illinois. Emig, a journalism graduate from the University of Wisconsin, was the first official head of journalism at Florida serving over twenty years in that position. Lowry had been a printer and newspaperman and was acting head of the journalism department during World War II. Jones was a University of Florida journalism graduate in 1937 before receiving a master's degree from the University of Wisconsin and teaching journalism at the University of Illinois after a stint in the Navy. Rae found his interview with the three faculty members the most interesting of his visit to Gainesville: "I didn't know a whole lot to ask them about the department and they didn't tell me a whole lot except what each one taught. The thing that struck me most was that Bill Lowry didn't seem to be much interested in any of the conversation and sat reading a newspaper during most of [the meeting]. I thought that pretty peculiar, but Bill was the kind who didn't care who the chairman was or who the dean was or the director, he would go along with any of it, do his job; he wasn't interested in any administrative details. Emig was very solicitous of anything I wanted but was an interesting and intelligent man. He was very good at English and at one time was writing editorials for the Daytona Beach paper while teaching. While in the Navy in World War II, he had the job of coding and decoding messages of the Navy fleets in the Pacific. I think they probably chose him because he was sharp, alert, and I am sure very conscientious. But after a few years, this nerve-racking and stressful job had its effect on him. When he came back to teaching, he was a great person to motivate students to think."

President J. Hillis Miller took a real gamble, perhaps one of the best gambles a university president ever took, in choosing a professional newspaperman instead of a professional educator, and that choice invoked some criticism. Miller chose Weimer because of his vigor, imagination, and determination, and his gamble would pay off in spades.[4] To the other academicians he might have arrived from another planet. He wasn't one of them. He was a journalist, a newspaperman. He may have been short on academics, but he was long on action.[5]

"Having accepted the position, Ruth and I drove to Gainesville in May to look for housing, leaving the kids with my parents on the farm," Rae continued. "We thought we would get an apartment for about a year, but there were no conveniently located apartments. The population of Gainesville at the time was about 26,000. Driving around with a real estate agent, we came upon a house under construction and only a few blocks from the U of F campus. The price of $15,000 was within our budget; we agreed to buy it right then and there. Our agreement to pay $4,000 down with the contractor paying the closing costs, was written on the back of a plain piece of paper. In 1949 very few of Gainesville's streets were paved so our new home at 2042 NW 7th Lane was on a sand street. We moved to Florida in the middle of June, staying at the Casa Loma Lodge on SW 13th Street until our home was ready in July of that year. We hadn't given any thought about blinds for the windows and had nothing to cover the windows at night when we turned on the lights. That summer of 1949, I wouldn't receive my first paycheck until the first of August so after paying the $4,000 down, it was mighty slim pickings the latter part of July as we just didn't have any money left."

Another reason the Weimers bought a home in northwest Gainesville was its proximity to an esteemed elementary school. "We bought the house that we did because it was only a block from J. J. Finley Elementary School [renamed Carolyn Beatrice Parker Elementary in 2020], which we found out was one of the highest rated elementary schools in Gainesville at that time. Both [of our children] went through the public schools entirely."

In Gainesville, the Weimer family became close to some of the other journalism school families, in particular John Paul Jones and his family. Rae said, "Paul and Marian Jones and their three children lived a few blocks from us and very early, almost from the time we moved in, we became close friends of the Jones family. Paul was a tremendous help to me in the office, since he had several years of teaching experience at the University of Illinois, which had a very good School of Journalism; Paul was also a graduate of the College of Arts and Sciences here at Florida in their journalism program. In addition, his local roots growing up in the area was another benefit to our family. Paul became a dear friend."

23 An Unlikely Department Head

Colleagues at the University of Florida with advanced degrees did not know what to make of this new hire who lacked even a bachelor's degree. "At my first faculty meeting (Journalism was still under Arts and Sciences), I was immediately confronted by an English professor who demanded to know how I wanted to be addressed. I said I didn't know what he was talking about. The professor responded, 'Do you want to be called doctor or mister or dean or what?' I said, 'How about just calling me Rae?' I had never thought anything about what people called me. Even the lowliest copyboy at *PM* just called me Rae. I knew I was the only person in that type of position without a degree. One doesn't brag about it, but a degree doesn't spell the difference between success and failure either."[6] To a man who had spent his entire adult life in the no-nonsense, unpretentious world of newspapers, such attention to protocol seemed strange. His response contributed to the legend of the degreeless dean.[7]

In a 1969 oral history interview with Dr. Samuel Proctor of the University of Florida's Department of History, Rae shared more of his impression about his recruitment: "I don't think [President] Miller had very much wholehearted support from academicians to bring someone out of the professional newspaper field. I think professors, by and large, are a little suspicious of newspaper people; in twenty years here, this has confirmed my earlier suspicions. They didn't understand newspaper people. They didn't trust them. And I don't think professors ever wanted to understand newspaper people. So, they had misgivings about my coming here. [Plus], I'd come from a paper that was the most liberal, outspoken paper in America. And this, of course, was contrary not only to the South, but to Southerners and conservatives that made up the majority of the university faculty at the time."

"Journalism, for many years, was a kind of stepchild at the university," Weimer told a reporter. "It had been kicked around and had no respect in the minds of the rest of the faculty. It didn't add much by my coming in. The powers of the university weren't pleased by the fact I didn't have a college degree.[8] It was clear from early faculty meetings I attended in the College of Arts and Sciences that there was a considerable question about me being a director of a school without a college degree. Perhaps I should finish my undergraduate degree, I thought. In the summer of 1950, I went back to Columbus, Ohio, registered at [The] Ohio State University in the School of Journalism with the intent to obtain my bachelor's degree. To my surprise, I found that their curriculum left a lot to be desired. The professor in charge of the summer program had me teaching the laboratory course in which I had enrolled since I had far more experience in the field of editing than anyone on their faculty. The most beneficial course I took that summer was one in political science covering the period from 1914 and World War I through the depression up until Roosevelt's election, one of the most exciting periods in our history and one very familiar to me. Six weeks later, back in Florida, I concluded it would be more to the School of Journalism's benefit if I would forego getting my degree.

"The summer when I went back for a six-week course at [The] Ohio State University's School of Journalism, I took Bill with me and stayed on the farm in Columbus. Mother, Dad, and Doc's family all enjoyed having him back. I think Bill got more out of his experience that summer than I got out of Ohio State. During the year we all lived on the farm, Bill had become thoroughly acquainted and happy with farm life. He loved the contact with the animals and machinery and following my dad everywhere. He really wasn't happy with the decision to move to Gainesville and welcomed the opportunity to return to the farm that summer of 1950."

24 A Department Becomes a School

Described by Judy Hamilton as a "Cinderella marking time in a garret,"[9] Florida journalism had humble origins indeed beginning in 1916. "Journalism at the University of Florida started with a single course in Agriculture Journalism in the Agriculture College," Rae explained. "For some twenty years the Department of Journalism had been sort of a stepchild, moved from a course in Agriculture, then to the College of Business Administration. When the chairman of the Department of Journalism at that time, Elmer Emig, and the Business College dean conflicted, journalism was moved into Arts and Sciences as a two-man department for about twenty years. I don't believe it had ever exceeded fifteen to twenty students. Journalism education at the college and university level was slow in coming to the South. Where it really grew was in the Middle West. Probably the first school of note was in Missouri, but Kansas, Indiana, Illinois, Ohio, Michigan, Minnesota, Nebraska, Texas (the only southern state), Colorado, and Oklahoma all had a department or school of journalism. Columbia University in New York had a widely known graduate journalism school—more widely known than its work deserved except maybe for those students who wanted to do research, but not much on a practical level. The South, the East, and the Ivy League schools all lagged behind in adding any special courses in journalism. Journalism was a department until I came. Creation of the School of Journalism as a unit of the College of Arts and Sciences by the Florida Board of Control came about with the cooperation of Florida's editors and publishers.

"When I arrived, John Paul Jones, who had gotten a master's degree and was teaching at the University of Illinois, had recently been hired as the third staff member; Bill Lowry was the second [hire]. The department was then housed in a temporary Army barracks, Building E, with only one classroom; an office for Emig, where he had a secretary; and, I guess, a room down the hall with Lowry and Jones. There were no typewriters and the only book in the place was a dog-eared dictionary that was years old. I could see why the newspaper people wanted a change because there was little similarity to what reporters would face working on a newspaper." Paul Jones recalled that he was "put in a room that used to be a restroom and every time they flushed the toilet next door, the water came through the pipes."[10]

Many issues confronted Rae as soon as he arrived at the university as he recalled, "We had no typewriters, obliging me to find some. I went down to an Air Force base in Orlando that first summer and bought fifteen of their old, surplus typewriters. We must have paid about $15 apiece; it then cost me that much to get them in working order. Securing books was a struggle; we had to fight the university because they didn't want us to have a separate library. Rather, the university wanted us to house our collection in the central library."[11]

"Meanwhile, I had to find a 'home' in Building E. One thing Elmer Emig had done for the department was to get a teletype that was in a sort of closet room, awfully small, and that is the only place they could find for me to have an office for the first month. The space was so small, you almost had to back out after a desk was installed. Knowing that the time to get what you need is when you are new, I immediately began to look around for more suitable space for what was now the School of Journalism. Our next location was another temporary building, also an old Army barracks–type building (The campus was full of those from World War II.), called Building K, with only 3,000 square feet of space and across the street from the gymnasium. Agriculture had one end of the building, but I did manage to secure two classrooms, more office space, and a little place for a library where Lowry had his office. We moved out of Building E in the fall of 1949."

Paul Jones in his history of journalism at the University of Florida described those early times: "There were problems with Building K. The building was unbearably hot in the summer. Weimer kept a thermometer on his office wall and when the gauge showed one hundred, he called the president's office and reported the temperature. This was a regular occurrence in the summer and eventually resulted in the school being moved to the football stadium in the fall of 1955. [Also], the walls were paper-thin and Rae Weimer was a 'shouter' on the telephone. When Ralph Page, dean of the College of Arts and Sciences, called he used to ask, 'Why don't you put down the phone, Rae? I can hear you without it!'"[12] His loud voice may have been a result of his newspaper days when he had to shout to be heard above the din of machines and other voices. A vivid memory Rae's daughter had from her childhood was of climbing the external stairs to Building K to retrieve her father at the end of the day and having to inhale the stench from the nearby animal research lab—she, too, was happy when the School of Journalism later moved out of Building K.

"One morning someone called me asking if I knew of a museum that would like to have one of the first presses in the state of Florida," Rae told oral history interviewer Samuel Proctor. "This old George Washington press had come down the Mississippi River from Cincinnati and across the gulf to St. Petersburg [where that city's first paper was printed on it]. I said, 'Yes, we're that kind of museum. I'll take it.' I had a university truck retrieve that 2,500-pound press, but our floor wouldn't hold it, so we had to shore up the floor to keep it from falling through.[13]

"The next thing I gave my attention to was a complete revision of the curriculum with the assistance of Paul Jones. At the time, journalism had courses entitled: Public Interest I, Public Interest II, and Public Interest III. I don't know what they taught in those classes. When I started, Lowry taught courses in typography or mechanics and some type of public relations; Emig continued to teach a course in public opinion; and Jones taught a magazine writing course—all in the original curriculum." Rae shared with Samuel Proctor that the department "had half a dozen pieces of type" for teaching typography. The professor had to hold the pieces up to show the students what type was. "I think Lowry built the stands and I bought some secondhand discarded type cases so each of our ten students at that time could stand at a type case. I felt it was important for students to get a feel of type to help them know why you couldn't get an extra letter in a line.[14]

"Jones suggested I teach the class for graduating seniors, which I named Applied Journalism. By November, I had told them all I knew about newspapers and told Jones that. He said I needed to make an outline early and stretch out all the material to cover the entire term. I struggled through that first semester, but it was rough. The curriculum had been strictly all journalism, which struck me as a serious mistake. We rewrote the entire curriculum—new titles, new content in all courses, and, of course, it was strictly all journalism then. That first year Paul Jones and I must have spent almost every evening back at the school in Building K working on that curriculum. Because we didn't have much time to get together in the daytime, we went back and worked on it about every night of the week except probably Friday, Saturday, and Sunday. And, of course, we couldn't offer any courses in the school until they were published in the catalog, and that meant any change we made for Fall 1950 had to be done very early in the spring. We also built the curriculum by requiring many hours outside the school. The following year we required a year of Political Science, a year of American History (the only school or college on campus to require the subject), a semester of Sociology, and a semester of Economics. The curriculum was continually broadened as time went on, adding more courses outside the School or College of Journalism."

A year after Rae arrived at the University of Florida, the new School of Journalism was accredited on its first try by the American Council on Education for Journalism, joining the other thirty-eight accredited schools in twenty-six states. This rating raised the standards in newspaper editing, radio, and public relations for excellence and service to Florida's newspapers and meant that Florida men and women would no longer have to leave the state to receive a quality education in journalism.

25 Recruiting Students

To address the needs of Florida's newspapers, those who were responsible for his hiring in the first place, Weimer wanted to work closely with them in his new position. One way to accomplish that was through summer student internships with actual newspapers to provide potential journalism students with direct job experience. Rae explained his unique approach to recruiting students: "Surprisingly, one of the things that made the school grow by leaps and bounds, stemmed from working with high school students throughout the state. When I came here, I knew the newspaper business better than I knew the business of teaching—that's an understatement. So, I decided if I was going to place my graduates, I needed to know the (Florida) newspapers. If I was going to make this school amount to anything I needed their support . . . it ought to be a two-way street. . . . So, I set out to go to every meeting, using any excuse I could, throughout this state to meet all the editors in Florida. I really drove a lot of miles."[15]

Previously an employee of a revolutionary newspaper, Weimer became a revolutionary by offering weekend workshops in journalism for Florida's high school students. "When I came to Florida there was a loosely knit high school journalism association for the southeastern states. I set out to organize a Florida High School Press Association strictly for Florida high schools.

"Within a couple of months after Florida announced it was establishing a School of Journalism at the University of Florida, Florida State University in Tallahassee also decided they would have a School of Journalism. There was considerable competition between the two universities as to who would manage the Florida High School Press Association. Since most of the teachers in Florida probably were graduates of Florida State University, they naturally had an allegiance to that university, and those who graduated from the University of Florida had leanings toward this university. As a result, there was some friction and competition as to who would run the state association. For the association of high schools all over the state to be successful, it was necessary to provide the leadership and financial support continuity to make it succeed. Therefore, in the first few years there were to be two officers, a director of the association and a secretary-type position. These jobs would alternate between the two universities. That is, one year the director would be at the University of Florida and the secretary at Florida State University and the next year they would reverse.

"High schools in the past had conducted workshops where schools in close proximity would get together on a weekend to hear speakers and meet with consultants to help them with their newspapers or yearbooks. Those meetings were also attended by businesses selling school jewelry as well as contracts to print yearbooks. So, Paul Jones and I started attending all of those workshops that we could; we were on the go almost every weekend in the fall. We talked to classes on topics such as advertising or the business part of running a newspaper. The seeds we planted really began to pay off.

"Florida State University did not do nearly as much promoting as we did. Soon we made a lot of friends throughout the state and within a couple of years, the daily newspapers responsible for bringing me to the University of Florida began to raise questions about the two universities going to the expense of starting two journalism schools. At that point a committee of newspaper editors was named to decide for the Board of Control. Both the director in Tallahassee and I made presentations about what we hoped to accomplish. After the presentations, the newspaper committee recommended to the Board of Control that the school at Tallahassee be abolished and some of their equipment sent to Gainesville and that there would be only one [state-supported] School of Journalism in Florida." [That was in 1959.]

"The decision to fund only one journalism school meant the full burden of running the state association fell to us. This association never collected any dues from the high schools; all expenses were borne by us. The high schools did pay for their students to attend. It was about that time that I hired John Webb from Ohio University to teach as well as to be the executive secretary of the High School Press Association. In the fall, the two of us would travel throughout the state on weekends putting on workshops for high school journalism students. Some of the better high school teachers around the state would occasionally come and speak. These inspirational workshops gave students a new kind of help in journalism. If they were unaware of what journalism was before or how to publish a high school newspaper, they sure knew after our workshops. When they graduated and were ready to go to college, they came storming into the University of Florida. Our enrollment jumped tremendously, becoming the fastest growing division, school, or college, at the University of Florida for at least ten or fifteen years.

"Another activity we instituted was our summer seminars on campus for students from all over Florida. One week was for students interested in newspaper journalism and the other week was for those interested in yearbooks. Probably more than a hundred students came each week. They stayed in university dormitories and in their free time, had access to the university pool and activities planned for them by the physical education department. Students enjoyed a pretty nice week and, again, thought of the University of Florida when planning where to attend college. John Webb oversaw these sessions although the support of our faculty and clerical staff was required to host the seminars every summer."

26 Finding Faculty

Rae had to convince the university of the benefits of expanding the school's faculty. "With this new influx of students, the school needed more staff," Rae said. "Adding faculty never did catch up with enrollment so that classes kept getting bigger and bigger. It was hard to convince the university we were as big as we were and that we needed more staff.

"Initially I envisioned the School of Journalism focusing on teaching reporters, which is what the association of newspapers had in mind when they advocated for my hire. I soon began to think that journalism was a larger field than just for newspapers and that students interested in the field of writing and communications needed an opportunity for a broader education than just training to be newspaper reporters. At that point, we branched into advertising as it related to newspapers, an expansion welcomed by the association of newspapers.

"Later it seemed to me that reporting was not going to be limited to newspapers alone. Radio, which preceded television by over twenty years, was doing some news reporting. A student by the name of Norman Davis registered in the College of Arts and Sciences to major in its Department of Speech because he wanted to go into radio and possibly television. It was when he came to me about taking some reporting courses to help him in radio that spurred me to consider offering a course in radio reporting. Paul Jones first taught the course while I searched for individuals familiar with radio and television. The university administration was receptive to this addition and transferred the part of Speech devoted to radio and television from Arts and Sciences over to the School of Journalism. Along with the transfer would come the two faculty members involved: Clark Weaver, who had been teaching radio classes with virtually no equipment, and Tom Batten, who was teaching television courses. However, Batten asked for a year's leave of absence to teach in Houston. In the meantime, I had found a replacement, Lee Franks, who had experience in television. When Batten's request for another year's leave was rejected, he quit, enabling me to appoint Lee to a permanent job.

"Other outstanding hires included Horance G. Davis, widely known throughout the state as 'Buddy.' A previous graduate of the University of Florida and a reporter for the *Times-Union* in Jacksonville before becoming capitol correspondent for the *Times-Union* in Tallahassee, Davis turned out to be one of the best teachers in the school. Another was Hugh Cunningham, then editor of the *Bryan Eagle* daily in Texas, who arrived in the late 1950s with valuable experience in both reporting and editing. As we grew in numbers, it seemed to me we needed to broaden the curriculum into advertising; for that job I hired Manning Seil whom Paul Jones had known at the University of Illinois.

"As our enrollment in broadcasting grew quickly, I immediately added two people Clark Weaver had known in Texas, May Burton and Mickie Newbill. Because some students wanted to do graduate work, it was necessary for me to look for someone with a doctorate. None of the people I had hired up until this time had a doctorate. That was when I hired Harry Griggs who was teaching in Indiana and had a PhD and Leonard Hooper from the University of Southern Illinois who also had a doctorate."

A 1959 *St. Petersburg Times* editorial said, "More priceless than gadgets [referring to the typewriters, supplies, and equipment Rae had to acquire in the early days], is the faculty of 18 which Director Rae O. Weimer gathered."[16] Once hired, there was little turnover in staff; they were described as satisfied and content. A *Florida Press* reporter explains why: "Weimer kept any hierarchical distinctions between instructors and administrators to a minimum, avoided friction among faculty members, and tolerated opposing viewpoints. His enthusiasm for tasks was infectious, prompting staff to work that much harder while enjoying their work."[17]

Pulitzer Prize winner and journalism faculty member H. G. "Buddy" Davis said of Weimer, "He does not bear grudges or bring pressures against anyone to change their mind. If there are any protests you never even know they exist, Weimer handles them so smoothly. I came here with a salary cut and a step down on the social scale . . . because of his enthusiasm and willingness to let people grow and his willingness to defend you, not stomp on you. That's why a lot of us came and stayed."[18]

Rae described part of his management strategy: "I operated with an open door policy so that I seldom missed a day when faculty and students were not coming and going in my office. That frequent contact with faculty helped me build a cooperative closeness in administration of the school."

27 Expansion Abounds

A pioneer in educational television in Florida, Weimer established a radio-television production center within the School of Journalism and Communications. The center taped educational programs for distribution to radio and television stations throughout Florida. Rae recounted his role: "Television, which had been ready to come on the market in the 1940s but was held back by World War II, now blossomed and grew nationally. My experience in broadcasting was nonexistent, but I knew we needed to add television to our broadcasting curriculum. Congress had allocated something like 250 channels reserved for educational television but no university had one yet. Iowa State University was granted a commercial channel and was offering some television broadcasting; then Michigan State added some courses in television, but had no on-the-air broadcasting. Syracuse University not only offered some courses in television but also had some on-the-air programming over the local television station. To gain knowledge in this budding field of television, [in the summer of 1953] I went out to Ames, Iowa, for a weeklong workshop on television and learned how they were running the first university television station in the country, WOI-TV. Next, was Michigan State for another workshop week. Finally, I went to Syracuse where I earned six hours of graduate credit without ever having a bachelor's degree! Next, I visited a number of commercial stations.

"Students were already preparing programs they rehearsed in one of the Building K classrooms under the direction of Lee Franks. On Saturday afternoon Franks and his students would drive to Jacksonville where Channel 4 would let us put on our half-hour program—our first introduction to on-the-air television. But we had to overcome all kinds of roadblocks. The university worried about liability regarding the students' travel as well as about what they might do or say. I spent untold hours day and night in 1953 working on the television project from application for the station to documenting qualifications of the staff, program material, and finances. The application itself was quite complicated and required hiring a representative in Washington to present our case to the Federal Communications Commission. That person cost us $100 per day for any day he worked on our behalf. Fortunately, the university funded the costs for the application process through a special allocation of funds since there wasn't enough money in the Journalism budget.

"Because we were dependent on appropriations from the state legislature every two years for our financial support, I sought out monetary support from the Ford Foundation, which had shown a great deal of interest in educational television or noncommercial television that would serve the public without depending on advertising for support. A group in Jacksonville was planning to apply for a noncommercial license but was not connected with any educational institution for what would be entirely a community effort. They, too, were seeking money from the Ford Foundation. The Ford Foundation finally decided they would donate $100,000 to the Jacksonville group and another $40,000 to $60,000 to us on the condition we would put in microwaves from Gainesville to Jacksonville in order that programs generated at the University of Florida's School of Journalism could be transmitted to Jacksonville. With my newly acquired knowledge of television, I successfully applied for one of the 250 educational television channels—Channel 5. Once more, additional space became necessary.

"Our next hurdle was finding space. I went to the business manager of the university, George Bowman, the kind of person who, if something needed doing, he did it. He didn't let red tape and a lot of bureaucratic gobbledygook stand in his way. Together, we considered the football stadium. Now, I was aware at the time that Ohio State had built dormitories for athletes under its stadium. Under Florida's football stadium, George and I found discarded athletic equipment, broken lawn mowers, and other sundry items. Plus, the space was several floors high. We decided to see if we could develop the stadium space. Even though I'd never built anything, even a doghouse, in my life, I got blueprints, measured off the space, and laid out how I would use it. We were able to convince WRUF radio station, which was already in cramped quarters, to put in about $100,000 of their money. The Athletic Department added money for office space at one end and additional money for a dormitory on the fourth floor for football players. Finally, the University of Florida Press was interested in taking over a section of the stadium and provided their money to that end.

"As it ended up, Journalism had television studios complete with control rooms on the first floor; offices, classrooms, and laboratories, including a typography lab with two presses, film processing darkrooms, and two photographic printing rooms, on the second floor; our radio center and three studios with two control rooms, plus a record library and more offices, on the third floor. After the floors and walls were in, the project stopped for lack of funds. We had to wait until the legislature met the next year to convince them to appropriate $100,000 to finish the area for Journalism. In all we had about 36,000 square feet of space. We moved from Building K to the stadium in 1955." Rae and faculty member Manning Seil designed new and more spacious student desks that were built for the school by shops at the university. Associated Press teletype machines on the second floor allowed students to edit wire copy just as they might later on a news desk.

"The football players in their fourth floor dormitory directly above our radio station became a problem," Rae reflected. "Fun-loving as they were, on one or two occasions, they turned on showers and plugged up drains with towels letting the water overflow into our radio studio. That stunt ruined or damaged some highly technical and expensive equipment and was the straw that broke the camel's back for me. I now had the ammunition I needed to press my claim for more space. The football players had to vacate their space, which the university gave to us as our school continued to grow rapidly in both faculty and students." With the new building, the School of Journalism's enrollment increased proportionally more than any other school or college at the University of Florida—from 97 to 150 students in 1955.

"Once our Channel 5 license was approved, I had to find a place to erect the transmitter tower. I simply thought we could add it behind the stadium (the most logical place) but discovered there was an emergency landing pattern there for Gainesville's airport. Land outside Gainesville known as Devil's Millhopper (a sinkhole) had been turned over to the university; they gave us sixteen acres for the tower. Glenn Marshall, general manager of Channel 4 WJXT in Jacksonville, was a great help in securing a transmission tower. (He also sent his engineers down to help design our studio.) About to put up a new 1,000-foot tower for his station, Glenn offered to give us the smaller tower he had been using. He did charge us around $3,000, and I still had to have it sandblasted, welded, and repaired. Our problems began when we dug the holes for the anchors, and found we were in water two feet down. We tried pouring concrete in the holes but it floated to the top and wouldn't set. Of necessity, we built cofferdams to keep out the water. We must have poured tons of concrete in those holes for our 300-foot tower. I think I wore the road out traveling there, sometimes twice a day in the summer of 1953 or 1954."

Still, with limited money Rae was restricted in the kind of equipment he could afford for the budding television station. The school found two small orthicon cameras in Indianapolis for $40,000 for the pair; they were not much larger than a movie camera. The new accommodations were not perfect as Rae explained, "In the stadium where we built our new quarters there were large concrete pillars supporting the stadium seating area above. When we had our first dedication of the television studio area, we invited all the television personnel management from Jacksonville, Orlando, and other stations as well as newspapermen. The first thing one of the television managers said was, 'Who was the knucklehead who built this studio with a pillar in the middle?' I had to explain that if you took out that pillar the whole stadium would collapse—there just wasn't any choice. The faculty started teaching television classes, using the radio center for a laboratory, and we were going 'great guns' in the broadcasting field even though we did not receive our license to go on the air until about a year later. We did some closed-circuit broadcasting even with the orthicon cameras in which we might give a lecture and put a TV-receiving set in the classrooms."

28 Creative Curriculum

With an increasing population of students, Journalism had to change its curriculum. "In the fall of 1956 we had far more students than we had anticipated or than we had faculty to teach." Rae said. "This was partly due to our work with the High School Press Association, our statewide workshops, and our summer seminars, all of which created tremendous interest all over the state for students to major in journalism and enroll at the University of Florida. This also benefited the school as the allocation of funds to the various schools and colleges was made on the basis of enrollment.

"In those days freshmen and sophomores registered in University College, but the School of Journalism was an upper division school that did not accept students until they were juniors. After creating great enthusiasm among the high school students with our seminars, I wanted to keep in touch with them as soon as they arrived and not wait until they had spent two years at the university before they got into journalism. To that end, we created the Survey of Communications course for freshmen, which they took as an elective in University College. The course was so appealing that other campus units, such as the College of Engineering, enrolled their students.

"Now with the orthicon cameras in place we put a receiving set in every classroom to accommodate the required freshman course, Survey of Communications, and taught that class by television. At the time no one was assigned to the class so I had one man from Journalism teach the printed media part, one man in Advertising teach that part, one from Broadcasting to teach Radio and Television, and one in Public Relations for that section. By the end of the year, I found very quickly that it would not work. The faculty was so steeped in their own field they tended to extoll its merits and denigrate other fields. At that point I decided to have Buddy Davis teach the entire class. First, he had to brief himself on the broadcast media in which he had no experience as well as prepare material that summer for advertising and public relations. At one point we had eighteen sections of that class. Buddy was able to put those lessons on tape to play at different times of day so it wasn't necessary to have all the classes meet at one time.

"A junior college in Ocala accessed the Survey of Communications course off the air and gave credit for it. That was after we had a permit in 1958 to go on the air with WUFT so anybody at home could listen, too. But the students in Ocala Community College had a receiver in their classroom and sent their papers to Buddy Davis to grade. Again, probably when they finished their junior college, they came to the University of Florida.

"To continue our philosophy of reaching out to lower division students, we created a course for sophomores called Writing for Mass Communications taught by Hugh Cunningham. It had some of the very basics of writing, grammar, spelling, and other fundamental skills we found weak among some of the incoming students. It wasn't long before Hugh had perfected his successful course and I thought we ought to print it for two reasons: one was we needed a printed outline and regular textbook and another was that if something happened to Hugh, no one else could really pick up and continue at his high-caliber level. When I proposed to Hugh Cunningham that he sit down and write the course, he thought it would be a good idea, but was too busy with his courses and never got around to it. I then put a tape recorder in his course for every lecture he gave for one semester, had it typed up, and the following summer I assigned him no classes so he could take this typed material and edit it into a textbook. The text appealed to other faculty on campus including the College of Engineering that enrolled many of their students in the course.

"I then took a copy of that paperback textbook printed in the large size of a notebook, to New York when I attended a meeting of the American Association of Schools and Departments of Journalism, of which I was president at the time. At this meeting of all the deans and directors of journalism institutions, they were fascinated with the outline I shared with them and suggested we should do a television tape of it. We never were able to tape it but the book sold to any number of other schools who wanted to adopt the course.

"A non-journalistic benefit of our license was our broadcasting a program in music and art appreciation to all the public schools in Alachua County. Each school put in a TV set to receive the program. Some of the high school art and music teachers would come to the studio to broadcast a lesson to all the schools at one time. Before that, many schools in the county could not afford art or music teachers. Sadly, that program was abandoned."

29 Most Acclaimed Journalism Students

By the 1960s the University of Florida School of Journalism was the fastest growing journalism program in the country.[19] After it later became a college, the College of Journalism and Communications' burgeoning enrollment made it the largest undergraduate college of its kind in the nation.[20] Not only did the University of Florida's College of Journalism and Communications surpass other journalism institutions in enrollment, but it excelled in creating quality students. Numbers of students alone are not a measure of a university college. Perhaps the more important measure is the quality of the graduates.

Rae expressed his pride in his students: "In 1960, the Hearst newspapers, which made up one of the larger chains of newspapers in America at that time, decided to start a contest and award cash prizes to students for their writing. These cash prizes for the students were matched by an equal sum sent to the school. In my time at the school, Florida won more of those national contests of writing than all the other schools in America put together. The top award would be presented in Washington, DC, by the president of the United States. The first year [1965] Florida won the national title, [and was named best journalism school in the country], I was invited to join President of the University J. Wayne Reitz, for that ceremony. Because it was Hugh Cunningham who had worked with the students all year in helping them finish and process their stories (only articles that had been published in a newspaper could be entered in the contest), I thought he should accompany us to the ceremony. President Lyndon Johnson made the presentation in the Rose Garden. What a thrill to be part of that ceremony! When President Johnson handed the medallion to President Reitz, it slipped out of its purple, velvet case and landed on the concrete at our feet. I suspect if you were to examine the medallion that today lies in the college trophy case, you would probably find one side with a slight dent."

This crowning achievement brought both state and national recognition. Congratulations poured in to Rae from all over Florida and nationally: bank executives; representatives to the US Congress; radio/TV stations; an AT&T executive in Washington, DC; lawyers; ministers; business leaders in the state; publishers; public relations directors; a Florida circuit judge; newspapers; colleges (including Oklahoma State University; Kearney State College; Lycoming College in Pennsylvania and the University of Florida); and the Rae O. Weimer chapter of Quill and Scroll at Chamberlain High School in Tampa, Florida. On its tenth anniversary, the School of Journalism and Communications was both nationally and internationally recognized. It was one of only forty-six accredited schools of journalism in the nation, ranking in the top ten among those.[21] The University of Florida had finished among the top three journalism schools for the four previous years. The only other school to come close to Florida's record at the time was two-time winner Nebraska.[22]

Part of the students' success rested with the outstanding faculty as Buddy Davis recalled: "I think the school flowered because we were fortunate enough to secure a dedicated faculty with a backbone of professional experience. Most were experts, and they spoke with authority. That means a lot to students."[23] Additionally, the relationship of faculty and students played a role in fostering excellence among both undergraduate and graduate students. Rae set the example as Paul Jones recounted in his history of journalism at the University of Florida: "[Rae ran] the School of Journalism and Communications with vigor and enthusiasm. He liked students and was always available to them at the office, at home, at night, on weekends, and during vacations. No student's problem was too small for him to handle. No job at the school was too insignificant for him to do. He arranged furniture in the classrooms, hauled mailbags up the stairs, opened newspapers, answered his own telephone, [and] mopped up the halls on a Sunday afternoon if a leaking pipe had flooded the place. He believed in instant communication with those he needed for information or advice."[24]

Rae never took sole credit for the college's many accomplishments. He even told President Lyndon Johnson in the White House Rose Garden ceremony that he was there only to receive the national writing championship medal his students had won. "The honor is not mine," he told President Johnson. "It belongs to the students and faculty who guided them."[25]

In the first seven years that the School of Journalism and Communications entered this national competition, it shared with the University of Nebraska the distinction of finishing higher than the other forty-eight accredited journalism schools that participated. During those first years, Florida and Nebraska were the only two schools whose students never placed below sixth place.[26] The College of Journalism and Communications continued its success throughout the 1970s and 1980s, finishing among the top ten schools twenty-five times in twenty-eight years. As the 1980s came to a close, the University of Florida had won the national title thirteen times.[27]

Twenty-five years after his death, the University of Florida College of Journalism and Communications Rae built continues to rank among the top ten in the nation. To cite a few of the recent rankings:

College Magazine's top ten journalism schools
(2019 as well as previous years)[28]

Niche A+, #6[29]

College Factual #9 (2022)[30]

PrepScholar #4 (2021)[31]

College Rank #2 (2022)[32]

The popularity of journalism and related fields was cited by the *College Gazette* in 2019: "Believe it or not, journalism is perhaps the most desired major in the country for today's millennial to pursue."[33]

In his interviews with Samuel Proctor, Rae estimated sixty to seventy-five Florida journalism students had "cracked the New York field. I came from New York, and you don't just walk in to New York and go to work."[34] These jobs were in public relations, advertising, and broadcasting more than newspapers, as there were no longer as many newspapers in New York. Rae believed practically every paper in Florida hired his graduates. Other former students became administrative assistants to congressmen in Washington, DC. Even the Army recognized their potential as Rae explained: "I started a program in which the Army sent their career officers [to Florida] to get master's degrees [in journalism]; some of them became top public information staff in the Pentagon. Others were hired in similar positions at Cape Canaveral." Rae felt the college made a great impact in journalism on the eastern seaboard.

30 Weimer Scholars

Rae was most proud of the success of his students, which he, in part, enabled. His open-door policy included not only staff but students as well. Whether students were not making the grade, had financial difficulties, were experiencing family troubles, or encountering any problem that might interfere with their academic success, Rae would take the time to listen and try to help them.

Hugh Cunningham also commented on Rae's great pride in remembering students he called "Weimer Scholars." They were the dozens of students on the verge of dropping out of college or having other difficulties that Rae encouraged to continue because he saw in them talents beyond mere academic ability. Regularly, many of them wrote to tell him of their successful careers. Here are some of their comments summarized by Jim Moorhead in the Fall 1994 issue of the *Communigator*:[35]

> When one graduate told Rae he was thinking of going to graduate school in journalism on the remainder of his GI bill, Rae asked, "What do you want to do that for? I think you ought to take that money and go to law school." William "Bill" Henry (JM 1950) did just that and went on to a stellar forty-year legal career.
>
> Another young man found higher admission standards at the university than he anticipated when he returned to Gainesville in 1965 from the Army. A mutual friend of Wayne Kestertson intervened on his behalf with Weimer; Wayne received his BS in advertising in 1966. He appreciated the "grand old man who refused to be limited by the university's rules. He gave us a chance to make something better of our lives . . ."
>
> Leonard Levy (ADV 1955) said, "I definitely qualify (as a Weimer Scholar)—would have never made it without Rae."

> Graduate Matt Schneider (JM 1967, TEL 1968) believed "the main goal of Rae Weimer and the faculty was to teach students HOW TO THINK. That is the most important skill I learned in my six years at UF."
>
> Treasured most by Pat Callan (ADV 1965) was the warm welcome Weimer gave him when Pat was desperate for an upper division opportunity after wasting too much time in University College and lacking the required second language courses. "Did I understand you right?" he queried Weimer. "You don't need a language in the College of Journalism?" Weimer smiled and responded, "Just one—American." "I love this man, I muttered to myself," Pat said.

Moorhead's column further described Rae as follows: "There was much to love . . . The regular-guy air. The rush of his pace that was never too hurried to include a hello. The bellowing to [his secretary] Katie (Lewis) from his office to hers and never mind an intercom. The voice that could be heard over a class break clear down to the street floor. The respect he earned for the way he ran things. His utter lack of self-importance. His flair for rescue."

31 The Degreeless Dean Steps Down

As Rae approached sixty-five years of age, when he would be required to relinquish his position as head of the School of Journalism, he focused on elevating the school to a college. He tells how this happened: "The school continued to grow, the faculty was enlarged, we had expanded our space to the stadium, and our students continued to win national prizes not only in journalism but also in advertising. My ultimate goal was to elevate the school to the status of a college, its rightful place among all the other units of the University of Florida. That finally occurred the first year Stephen O'Connell replaced Dr. Reitz as president of the University of Florida [in 1967]. The Florida legislature had created the School of Journalism [and now created the College]. I suggested to President O'Connell that it was time for the college to have a new dean and that I would step down. John Paul Jones succeeded me as dean of the college. I had served as the founder and chief administrator of the School and College of Journalism and Communications for nineteen years." By now a full professor, Rae was able to enjoy the prestige and salary benefits of being a dean for only one year. In 1967, Weimer became the only college dean in the nation without a college degree before stepping down in June 1968.[36]

Following are many firsts achieved during Rae's nineteen years as head of journalism at the University of Florida:

> The school became the fastest-growing journalism unit in the nation and the fastest-growing of all the units at the University of Florida.
>
> The school inaugurated closed-circuit television teaching in Florida.
>
> The school had the first nationally accredited professional journalism and communications programs in Florida—and maintains that "first" still.

The school installed the first chapter of Theta Sigma Phi, a national honorary fraternity for women, in Florida, and the first chapter of Kappa Tau Alpha, a national scholarship fraternity for journalism students.

The school cosponsored a half-million-dollar project for filming a high school chemistry course.

The school was designated in 1959 by the Board of Control as the only state-supported School of Journalism in Florida.

The school set up a Radio Center to provide the radio stations of the state with program material produced at the University of Florida.

The school provided the Florida Scholastic Press Association with state headquarters and provided the office with a director.

The school established the High School Press Institute, a summer program to help train high school newspaper and yearbook editors and other staff members.

In 1961, a branch library was established in the school, even though it was called a "Reading Room."

About this same time, 1961, the school set up its first photography laboratory and began teaching photojournalism.

The school was the most consistent winner in the history of the Hearst writing contests when Weimer was required to relinquish his deanship upon turning sixty-five.

After stepping down as dean, Rae did not retire from working but continued to give his time and skills to the University of Florida. "In June 1968, I left the college as dean and President O'Connell appointed me as his special assistant, moving me to yet another office on campus—in Tigert Hall," Rae said. "The first assignment I had in arriving at Tigert Hall was to arrange for the inauguration of President O'Connell. Well, they couldn't have picked anyone who knew less about inaugurations of college presidents than I did. I contacted all the speakers personally, which was quite an undertaking, and the ceremony was a success. In addition to assigning me the inaugural job, O'Connell made me chairman of the Honorary Degree Committee. Other duties included managing the supervision of the concessions on campus, helping to obtain funds for campus projects, such as purchasing all new uniforms for the Gator Marching Band, writing speeches, preparing material for press conferences, and attending events on behalf of the president."

Rae and Max Lerner, his friend and colleague from *PM* days, kept in touch over the years. Another of Rae's duties as assistant to the university president was to head up the Honorary Degree Committee. Writing to Lerner in October 1972 about Lerner's nomination for an honorary degree from the University of Florida, Rae explained his role: "I prepare material and take it to the committee on honorary degrees. Actually, I have much more influence in this committee than just being a member. After the committee makes a recommendation, I take it to the University Senate. With the Senate's approval, also a recommendation, it is sent to the Regents for final approval." Rae secured Lerner's talents as a guest lecturer by bringing him to the University of Florida on several occasions including as commencement speaker on December 16, 1972, when Lerner also received the honorary degree LittD, from the university.

"Early in 1973, there came across my desk the announcement of a retirement dinner for faculty members in the College of Agriculture," Rae recalled, "and it struck me as a particularly nice thing to do for faculty who were retiring. I discussed with O'Connell that we ought to do something for the whole university whereby the retiring faculty would be honored. At the mandatory retirement age of seventy, I left the President's Office in July 1973, returning to the College of Journalism and Communications to work on fundraising for a new building but stayed only until the end of the year when I became more active again in pursuing a retired faculty organization. A number of subcommittees came together in January 1974. We decided to call our fledgling organization the Retired Faculty Association; I was named temporary president. That November the name was changed to the Retired Faculty of the University of Florida and incorporated in Tallahassee. At our first annual meeting in May 1975, I was elected president of the newly chartered organization for the University of Florida's retired faculty.

"The five years working as O'Connell's special assistant were stimulating, exciting, and a marvelous way to conclude my career at the University of Florida. I had originally intended, when I stepped down as dean, to go back to teaching, but I think it was better for me and better for my successor that I did not return to the college. Because I had founded the school, which then became a college, every person there had been hired by me. If I had stayed on as a faculty member, it would have been inevitable that some of the faculty would have come to me about problems they might not want to talk to the new dean about. I think it is always better for the incoming dean to set up his own operation."

Former University of Florida president Stephen O'Connell recounted his choice of Rae as his special assistant: "One of the wisest, most rewarding decisions I made as president here was to ask Rae to become my special assistant . . . when he retired as dean! The great respect held for him by the media—many, many his former students—enabled him to speak for me and interpret the actions of the university from a perch no other person could have occupied . . . More importantly, he gave wise counsel and was my warm and loyal friend in the most tumultuous years endured by university presidents everywhere. He helped to make life livable."[37]

Although fully retired from academia and now dean emeritus, Rae would not sit idle. He needed to be engaged with people; he wanted to serve his fellow man. The next chapter in his life would find this man of boundless energy continuing to be active in his community as long as he was physically able.

PART V

Seeing the World

32 Dean of Travel

Rae's adventures and his love of travel started shortly after he married Ruth: "The first trip abroad that Ruth and I took was on a banana boat to Honduras on a standard shipping line later taken over by the United Fruit Company. On the way we stopped in Santiago, Cuba, where we tourists were all taken to the Bacardi Rum factory. That night we sailed on down to Honduras. The next day we took a boat cruise upriver to the interior where the banana groves were." After this experience, the inquisitive Rae relished traveling abroad, learning about new cultures and seeing historical sights, enjoying this "hobby" for four decades.

Another early travel experience Rae recounted involved the opening of a new airline route. The American Overseas Airline (AOA), which had previously been known as American Export Airlines (AEA), flew from the United States to Europe beginning in 1945 until 1950 when AOA merged with Pan American. American Overseas Airlines' *Flagship Reykjavik* (an unpressurized Douglas DC-4S) was the first scheduled service linking the United States and Scandinavia with Iceland. Another first for the flight was the invitation for Members of the Aviation Writers Association and other journalists to participate in an inaugural flight of a US overseas airline.

"I have to recount an experience I had in March 1947 when export lines were opening up an airline route between New York and Stockholm," Rae said. "To mark the opening, a planeload of New York City newspapermen flew to Iceland to meet another planeload of Swedish newspapermen flown in from Stockholm for the ceremonies. On our trip from New York to Iceland we had to stop and refuel in Gander, Newfoundland, before continuing over the northern Atlantic. While flying over the northern Atlantic, the water was a clear blue strewn with large, white icebergs floating below us. We were told before we came that we should bring tuxedos for the formal embassy events, but I never wore mine [the one that gave Rae the opportunity of his life—meeting his wife, Ruth].

"The thing that amused me was after we got out over the water, we had a demonstration from the stewardess on how to get into a Mae West (life) vest in case the plane went down, and we were plunged into the water. What was ironic about it was that if you had to get out in that water, freezing cold as it was, you probably wouldn't live over fifteen minutes whether you had a Mae West on or not! Maybe they thought the vest would keep your body afloat until they found you dead.

"For a week we were wined and dined and briefed at the various embassies. We were able to experience the hot springs of boiling hot water bubbling out of the ground that the government tapped to transport down to Reykjavik for the city's hot water radiators. Many of us took off our shoes and socks, rolled up our pants, and waded in a stream of warm water amidst high snowbanks on each side of the stream. Our return flight was delayed a week when a blinding snowstorm left us snowbound in Reykjavik. Most of us didn't mind—I didn't want to leave in the first place. Finally, we departed at 8:00 a.m. in our bus led by a four-wheel-drive Army munitions vehicle clearing a track in the road completely covered in snow drifts. However, we did not arrive until dark at the airport in Keflavik. It took three attempts to take off and rather than the regular refueling stop in Gander, we had to detour farther north in Canada to Goose Bay, Labrador. A military plane had crashed trying to land in Gander and there were some fatalities. After refueling in Goose Bay, we continued on to our destination, New York City. A great experience all in all."

International travel on a more regular basis for Rae did not begin until almost a decade later. When the European Traveling Seminar of Copenhagen sought an outstanding educator with newspaper background to head its 1956 journalism tour abroad, it chose the University of Florida's director of journalism, Rae Weimer, to lead the tour. As Rae remembers, "A sideline that brought me great pleasure was leading tours and traveling abroad for thirty-plus years. I took my first trip to Europe in 1956 when I was asked to lead a group of twenty-two college students [only two of whom were boys], two professors, two ministers and their wives. In those days, college girls were just beginning to travel abroad and it seemed the parents were more comfortable if their children were chaperoned, especially by a college professor. As it was my first experience, first trip to Europe, and first time leading a group, I must say I had considerable anxiety and foreboding about going. Despite my misgivings, all went well. As this was before the modern day of hordes descending on Europe, we enjoyed rare experiences like walking right up to the stones at Stonehenge, which today are cordoned off. I found foreign travel highly educational and fascinating, whetting my appetite for future travels.

"A couple from Copenhagen, Denmark, owned the travel agency that organized my first tour known as 'the Traveling Seminar.' Arne Sorensen, one of the owners, was a famous Danish politician and World War II resistance fighter. Arne Sorensen had been an organizer and leader of the resistance movement in Denmark during World War II. Because the Germans placed a bounty on Arne, he was moved every few days from attics to cellars to wherever his countrymen could hide him for fear that the occupying Germans would find him. On more than one occasion, the Germans were so frustrated with their inability to locate Arne, they would take hostages into the town square and shoot them in trying to force the populace to give Arne up to them. After the war, he was a member of the Danish Parliament. While our group was touring Copenhagen, we visited a war memorial museum that included depictions of the resistance movement and the part Arne played."

Driving the mountain roads in Europe exhilarated Rae, particularly the highway past the Franz-Josefs-Höhe glacier where their bus made a stop. Rae recalled his experience that cold and snowy day, "The girls had purchased a pair of lederhosen, short leather pants, for me. That morning at breakfast they had insisted I wear them that day. So, like a good sport, I did. But when we got to the glacier and got out in that cold wind and snow, I darned near froze! While the girls were drinking hot chocolate at the inn after our walk, I dashed back to the bus, got my suitcase, and put on some decent clothes."

One of the stops the Traveling Seminar made was Salzburg, Austria. Rae recounted an episode that upset the ministers in his group. "The night before we left Salzburg, the girls wanted to go down to the wine cellar where a band was playing. As chaperone, I went wherever the girls went. It wasn't until after midnight that we all went up to bed. Anyway, the minister heard about our evening and at breakfast the next day began upbraiding the girls about being down in the den of iniquity. As college students, the girls did not appreciate being preached to.

"There were really no problems until we got to Munich to hear a lecture at a Hofbräuhaus. Well, the bus broke down and the students had a beer or two (maybe three or four) while they were waiting for the bus to be fixed. Anyway, we finally got the bus fixed. The girls boarded the bus carrying steins of beer. As we took off on the Autobahn, the girls wanted me to turn on the radio to dance in the aisles and have fun. Soon, they needed a rest stop, but we discovered there were no rest stops on the Autobahn; so, I had the bus driver stop and the girls went off into the woods. Needless to say—the Baptist preacher and his wife weren't happy about any of this. By the time we arrived in Cologne, where the two Danes were to meet us and give us some money they owed us, the preacher had a talk with the Danes about my taking the girls into a wine cellar, letting them drink beer, and stopping along the road for toilet facilities, all of which they thought was improper. The preacher and his wife said, 'You have to send Weimer home. He isn't fit to be in charge of a tour like this.' The kids heard about this and demanded that the preacher be sent back home instead. Arne told them, 'I'll give you your tickets right now and you can go home. We aren't going to send Weimer home!'" [Both Weimer and the preacher stayed.]

Rae related another anecdote about that trip to Bill Adams for his November 25, 1965, article, "Weimer's Bag Packed with Travel Experience," published in the *Florida Business Journal:* "In Paris, the two [college] boys on the trip decided they wanted to take a French flag back home for a souvenir, so they found a flag one night and shinnied up the pole to get it. Since they couldn't speak or read French, they didn't realize the flag was flying in front of a police station. They got caught and the police sent for me. Well, I didn't speak French either, but I talked them into letting the boys go free with just an apology—in English, of course.[1]

"And then there was a problem with one of the girls. She was wealthy and when she went shopping, she went shopping. She found some parasols and liked them so much she bought a dozen. I didn't object to that, but when she came back to the hotel with a live French poodle puppy, I had to put my foot down. I went with her to the shop where she had bought the puppy and convinced the owner that there was no way the puppy could survive a bus tour of Europe, so he took the dog back and returned her $90."[2]

Rae was fortunate to begin his travels at a time when the main tourist attractions in Europe were not mobbed by masses of people. A real cultural highlight for Rae was one which is no longer available to tourists—the opportunity to view the original Lascaux Caves before they were closed to the public in 1963 in order to preserve the paintings. Discovered in 1940 by some boys when their dog fell into a hole, the caves' famous prehistoric drawings greatly impressed Rae: "I remember paying someone at a small farmhouse to enter the cave lit with lights strung with wires along the ceiling. The art was extremely realistic paintings of animals, some depicting action in a way I had never seen before.

"Our return voyage from that first European tour was aboard one of Holland America's older and smaller ships, *The Waterman,* a US built Victory class troop transport ship purchased in 1947 by the Dutch government and later rebuilt for passenger use," Rae remembered. "With no individual cabins on board, I was berthed in a double-deck iron bed in a cabin for eight men. Almost every day it rained or stormed with half the passengers sick. The crossing was the most disagreeable trip I ever took on water. When we docked in New Jersey, I was so happy to disembark." Needless to say, that was Rae's only trip chaperoning a group of coeds.

Thus began Weimer's "hobby" of leading tours around the globe. On the next European Traveling Seminar in 1961, Rae was able to take his wife and two children who were seventeen and fifteen, along with a few other families with children of similar ages on a monthlong tour. Of the thirty-three participants, a third were teenagers. Rae's daughter, Ann, caught the travel bug and thoroughly enjoyed the opportunity to interact with young people her age and not just the adult participants. She found the exposure to the arts, architecture, historical structures, and foreign culture more educational than anything she could have learned from a book. A return voyage on the *Nieuw Amsterdam* with her mother was Ann's first of many future ocean cruises. Son Bill wrote a piece for his high school newspaper, the *Hurricane Herald,* that fall of 1961. Like his sister, Bill found the trip "a wonderfully enriching experience and educational summer."

"I'm not bragging, but I built up a tremendous following soon after that first trip with the kids to Europe," Weimer told Bill Adams. "At first, I would come up with the idea, then I would contact a friend in New York who helped me plan the trip and another friend with Pan American Airlines who would help with the air travel."[3] Later, Rae found that because of a litigious society and the risk of mishap or accident, it was prudent to work through local travel agencies because they carried liability insurance—usually Holbrook Travel in Gainesville, an agency Rae found knowledgeable, reliable, and creative in planning itineraries.

Hugh Cunningham, a journalism professor and occasional traveler with Weimer, acclaimed how generous Rae was with his time and counsel regarding travel, which was always provided free of charge. He never received a salary for leading his "Weimer Tours" although the travel agency paid for Rae's and Ruth's passage.[4]

"Marco Polo of the jet set" was how Presbyterian minister Ross Mackenzie described Rae, further noting that wherever he traveled, Rae was always interested in the larger human family. The minister said of Weimer in his presentation of the Service Above Self Award to Rae on January 10, 1989:

> Rae never seems to get out of bed anything but mirthful and in good spirits—and this despite much pain in recent years. He seems to be able to click his camera at more people, animals, and buildings than anyone else I know. One story I do want to tell about his travels. Rae was invited into a second grade class to show some slides of the animals he had seen on his world travels. The class was invited, following his presentation, to write an essay on "My Favorite Animal." As they were all writing, Rae walked among them. [One girl] looked up at him. "How do you spell 'sex'?" she asked innocently. Somewhat puzzled, Rae said, 'S-E-X.' He went to the teacher and reported the inquiry from the innocent. The teacher then went to her and asked why she had asked to spell that word. "Well," she said, "my favorite animals are insects, and I only know how to spell 'in.'"

Bill Adams claimed in his *Florida Business Journal* piece in November 1965 that Rae was becoming known around Gainesville as the "dean of travel experts."[5] Adams added, "With forty-plus years of travel experience to almost every corner of the globe, Weimer celebrated his eighty-second birthday on a cruise through the Panama Canal." Sadly, Rae's battle with cancer forced him to give up not only his volunteer work but, after more than thirty years, organizing and leading group tours around the world.

PART VI

Retirement Years

33 Community Service

The University of Florida had a rule that a dean had to retire at sixty-five but could continue in another capacity until reaching the mandatory retirement age of seventy for all university positions. For Rae Weimer, retirement did not mean sitting back on his laurels. When Rae left his position as special assistant to the president of the university, Stephen O'Connell, he was not ready to call it quits. He enjoyed serving his community and did not want that to stop so he focused on volunteering. He now had a chance to become even more active in his community—his church, the local health-care system, the retired faculty association—as well as continue to travel the world with his wife and friends. He always answered the call, putting others' needs above his own. Rae supported important causes he believed in and the people he held dear—family, friends, colleagues, tour participants, church members, and community members with whom he served. "I'm busier now than when I got paid for it," Weimer said, laughing in an interview with a newspaper correspondent. "Being busy is what keeps me going. I think people who retire and sit around, soon die . . . People ought to do things . . . rather than sit around vegetating. God put me on this earth to do things and not sit around the piazza or the porch or somewhere and guzzle beer. If I have any particular goal, it is to continue as long as I can to be useful to people, to serve the community. I believe in service."[1]

Soon after he arrived in Gainesville in 1950, Rae began his volunteer work when he headed the publicity division of the Red Cross drive in Alachua County. His volunteer work continued to expand alongside his journalism career. As Rae worked tirelessly on behalf of his community, his service included cochairing a task force on crime in Alachua County, leading a county commission on economic development, founding the first United Community Fund in Gainesville, serving on the board of the American Red Cross, becoming a founding member of the board and acting as secretary for the Santa Fe Health Care, and more. He continued to be an active member of the Kiwanis service club and the First Presbyterian Church where he was an elder and deacon for many years. If there was a chance to better his community, Rae was there volunteering.

Volunteerism for Rae included participating in his children's lives, despite his busy career schedule. For three years from 1953 to 1955, Rae served as Cubmaster for a Gainesville church–sponsored Cub Scout Pack of which his son, Bill, was a member. Each year, this pack won first place in regional competitions. Bill's other fond memories of his father include: playing catch in the backyard despite Rae's crippled right arm; going fishing with his dad and Paul Jones; accompanying Bill to the nearby elementary school to shoot basketballs on an old wooden backboard; Rae's putting up a basketball hoop at the end of a new concrete patio so Bill could practice shooting; Rae and Ruth both driving Bill across Gainesville to watch him play in a YMCA basketball league; Rae's coaching Bill's Little League team; and Rae's support of Bill playing football for one year including advocating for Bill to wear a face mask (he was the first player to get league permission to wear one).

Ann, too, remembered her father's involvement in her life, "Although he had to work long hours, Dad took the time to attend my activities from taking me and a group of cheerleaders to sporting events, attending my piano and dance recitals, and going to other sundry activities."

A leader in improving the health care of Alachua County citizens at a price they could afford, Rae was a proponent of converting Alachua General Hospital from a for-profit entity to a not-for-profit health-care facility. In 1978, Rae became a member of the founding board of directors serving continuously for the next six years. A result of the change in status to a nonprofit hospital was the conversion of a million-dollar loss into more than a half-million-dollar surplus—by the time Weimer left the board, net revenues were more than $3 million.[2] In 1982, Santa Fe Health Care assumed the operation of Alachua General Hospital. This health-care system also benefited from Weimer's involvement as a charter member.

After an extensive search for an individual with impeccable integrity, Weimer was chosen to chair the Alachua County Development Policy Advisory Committee. The Alachua Board of County Commissioners had been concerned with polarization between unfettered growth and no-growth factions with previous meetings full of acrimony. They needed to find a nonpartisan, untainted person whom either side could trust. Leveda Brown, county commissioner chairperson, told Hugh Cunningham, "Rae Weimer emerged head and shoulders above everybody else. And, though at considerable personal monetary expense to himself and his sacrificing some long-planned personal endeavors, he accepted."[3]

One aspect of retirement that Rae appreciated was sleeping late rather than waking at the crack of dawn for work. He also felt that he might no longer fit in as well at the university due to bureaucratic changes, "I'd go crazy there now, because you can't run your own show. You have committees deciding things now—it's no longer up to the individual. On a newspaper you rise and fall on yourself. And in an administrative position you have to be able to make quick decisions to put people into action."[4] He did look forward to staying in touch with students, but bemoaned the fact that he no longer knew many of them due to the large number of students now enrolled.

34 Honors and Awards

In 1968, the faculty of the University of Florida College of Journalism and Communications sought an honorary degree for Dean Weimer but were thwarted in that attempt because he had become special assistant to President O'Connell and university policy prohibited such an award for someone employed by the university. The faculty again sought an honorary degree "commensurate with his service to the University of Florida and the State of Florida" for Dean Emeritus Weimer after he fully retired in January 1974.[5] "The first week of January 1974 saw my retirement from all duties at the University of Florida," Rae said. "At the end of that year, the university honored me by conferring on me an honorary degree."

The new dean, John Paul Jones, said this at the award ceremony: "I present Rae O. Weimer, native Nebraskan and adopted son of Florida, for the honorary degree of Doctor of Letters. Without benefit of a college degree, Rae Weimer pioneered journalism education in Florida, and shaped one of the most innovative journalistic endeavors attempted in the twentieth century. His career has included almost a half century of dedicated service to journalism including more than twenty years as a practicing newspaperman in the Midwest and later in New York City."[6]

When University of Florida president Robert Q. Marston conferred Rae's honorary doctor of letters, he commented: "Rae O. Weimer, your activities have enriched journalism and journalism education in this nation and this state. As a news gatherer, writer, and newspaper executive, you have been enthusiastic and innovative. As a teacher, counselor, and university administrator, you brought warmth, understanding, and friendship to the classroom and council chambers."[7]

Not only did the University of Florida honor Rae Weimer by bestowing on him an honorary doctorate, but numerous community organizations also recognized his contributions. Rae received two citations from Florida governors for service to the state. One high school in West Palm

Beach and one in Tampa named their honorary Quill and Scroll chapters in honor of Rae Weimer for his work on behalf of students. The Florida Press Association, Florida Association of Architects, Florida Scholastic Press Association, Florida Outdoor Writers Association, Florida Public Relations Association, and a number of honorary organizations at the University of Florida awarded him other citations of honor for outstanding service. He was seen as "a man who values the idea, a man who cherishes the individual, and a man who seeks the truth."[8]

Next is a more complete list of honors bestowed on Rae Weimer.

1966 Elected president of the American Association of Schools and Departments of Journalism.

1968 Honorary membership in the University of Florida Alumni Association based on his record of service to the university.

1968 Alpha Delta Sigma Aid to Advertising Education Award (AIDE): One of six national winners of the first annual AIDE award by this national professional advertising fraternity for outstanding support to the local chapter and to the advertising program at its university over the years. Rae had been initiated into his local chapter in 1950.

1970 Nominated for the 1970 edition of *Outstanding Floridians* because of his accomplishments and service in making Florida a leading state in the nation.

1980 Outstanding Alumni Award, Kearney State College. "Of the five honorees at Kearney's Diamond Jubilee awards, I was the only one who did not have a degree," Rae said.

1986 *Gainesville Sun* annual Community Service Award. A dozen letters of recommendation poured into the *Gainesville Sun* nominating Rae Weimer for its annual Community Service Award.

1989 E. T. York Service Above Self Award from the Rotary Club of Gainesville that "recognizes the individual who has rendered outstanding, dedicated, unselfish service, which has enhanced the personal quality of the lives of local citizens."[9] Another past Rotary president, Randy Caton, noted Rae was "just head and shoulders above the other applicants. For the man to develop the School of Journalism and Communications without a college degree himself was just amazing."[10] Ross Mackenzie, senior minister of the First Presbyterian Church spoke on behalf of Rae at the January 10, 1989, ceremony saying, "A good society bestows honor on those who have taught it the noblest human lesson: the dignity of service. The service we render for others is the rent we pay for our room on this earth and Rae Weimer has overpaid his rent. Rae Weimer is the most self-giving, generous-hearted man our family knows. Rae called me this morning and said: 'Before you say anything about my accomplishments, be sure to tell them that they are not mine. No one ever does things alone. You work with others. The university and the community have done a lot for me.'"[11]

1990 Florida Newspaper Hall of Fame sponsored by the Florida Press Association, for individuals who displayed outstanding service in the field of newspaper journalism in Florida. The Hall of Fame was established in 1988.

1992 University of Florida Presidential Medallion.

Outstanding Service Award from Florida Student Society of America.

State Press Award for Outstanding Service in Journalism Education in Florida.

35 Weimer Hall

Another honor for the founder of Florida journalism was in the works. Rae said, "My successor as dean, Paul Jones, had started a program [in 1968] to raise private funds to build a new building for the college that had completely outgrown the space in the stadium and asked me to assist in that endeavor. Of the many problems in the stadium, one of the worst was that every time it rained, some of the rooms were sure to have water leaking into them. And it was impossible to operate with delicate, expensive television and radio equipment getting ruined when it got wet. One of the reasons I did not continue with the fundraising project was that I did not particularly enjoy such activity, but did it at Paul's request and because it was something that I knew had to be done. As it turned out, about $2 million was raised in private funds, the second largest journalism endowment in the nation." One of those sources was a $1 million donation from the Gannett Foundation of Rochester, New York, with the stipulation that the college raise another $750,000 from the communications industry to help pay for the building.[12] Florida newspapers and broadcasting agencies, as well as alumni, donated another million.[13]

Rae continued, "President [of the University of Florida] at the time, Robert Marston, put the building project in the university budget resulting in the State of Florida financing the new building. The state funding along with the privately raised funds made up probably one of the largest endowments of any college of journalism and communications in the country. Ironically, the site for the new building was where the School of Journalism's location in barracks Building K had stood years before.

"Another endowment in support of students came quite unexpectedly," Rae said. "During my years of working on Scripps-Howard newspapers, I had several occasions to interact with Karl Bickel, general manager of United Press. About the time I came to Florida, he retired from United Press and moved to Sarasota. Hearing that he was in Florida, I invited him to come to Gainesville to talk with our students. Students were fascinated by his stories of his early-day reporting, of covering famous murder cases, and other unusual stories. Karl thoroughly enjoyed his contact with the students. He did one thing that amused me when he came to the campus. He and his chauffeur would spend the night at a motel for which I received a bill. In those days there were no funds available for such guest lecturer expenses, so when Karl came up I had to pay the motel personally. Years later after I retired as dean, Paul Jones called me up and told me a lawyer representing Karl's estate after he died, informed Jones that Karl made an annual bequest of $25,000 for scholarships to graduate students. In the end, my payment of his motel expenses had greatly benefited the college."

When it came time to name the new University of Florida College of Journalism and Communications building, there was a problem. To avoid any future embarrassment, the Florida Board of Regents had a precautionary practice that buildings within its nine state university campuses would not be named for living individuals. Yet, an exception was made in the case of Rae Weimer.

To honor Rae Weimer during his lifetime, two state senators successfully sponsored bills in the Florida legislature to circumvent that rule. The new building was named Rae O. Weimer Hall and dedicated in October 1981, when he was seventy-seven, making him one of the few individuals to have a building at the University of Florida named for him while he was still living. When asked about this tribute, Weimer replied, "You feel pretty humble about that. So many other people had so much to do with it; it wasn't me alone. But you feel pretty proud, too."[14]

Unfortunately, Ruth did not live to see Rae receive the honor of having a building named for him. Not long after he retired, adversity confronted Rae again when he lost the most important person in his life, his wife Ruth, in 1979 at the age of sixty-nine. Hugh Cunningham remarked that together Rae and Ruth "led an exemplary married life, reared children who live exemplary lives . . . and served as role models . . . to the hundreds whose lives they touched."[15] Although Rae missed her more than he could express, he continued serving the community, leading his tours, and socializing.

"At the time of Ruth's death in 1979, former president of the university, Stephen O'Connell, gave funds in her honor for the construction of a trophy display area in the new college building; that area was dedicated at the building-naming ceremony," Rae said. "Ruth was a big, big help in the school in a kind of behind-the-scenes way."[16] When the Weimers moved to Gainesville," Rae explained, "there were very few women interested in the profession [of journalism]. Because of her background in journalism, she stepped forward as a volunteer to organize the professional societies, which helped to gradually attract more women to our field. She organized the student chapter of Theta Sigma Phi, a national honorary fraternity for women in journalism that later became the Association for Women in Communications. As a member of the National League of American Pen Women, Ruth organized and served as charter president of the Gainesville chapter. She served as columnist and women's editor for the *Gainesville Sun* (1950–55 and 1962–66)."

O'Connell said of Ruth at the dedication: "It would not be right if in this building named for Rae no mention were made of his full partner, Ruth. They lived their lives in support of each other as few couples do. She did not resent, but shared, his commitment to the faculty and students of the college and served as advisor to student groups. . . . I remember with deep gratitude the many kindnesses and wise counsel she extended my wife when we came to the university."[17] While Ruth, too, served the Gainesville and university communities as women's editor of the *Gainesville Sun*, other journalism organizations, and her church, her first priority was always supporting Rae and her family. This journalistic pair made a widely heralded contribution to journalism in Florida.

One of the college's journalism students, Jeff Hardison, interviewed Rae around the time of the Weimer Hall dedication, asking him if there had been any disappointments in his career. "I don't know of any disappointments in my career. I'm basically an optimistic person. I'd rather look to tomorrow than worry about what happened yesterday. Sure, there are a lot of things that set you back a little, but I think character for all of us is built on adversity to some degree. You wouldn't have the strength to do the things you do and work as hard as you do, if you didn't have some adversity. I suppose the greatest loss I ever had was my wife ['s death]."[18]

"Seven years after I received the honorary doctorate," Rae recounted, "the University honored me again by naming the new $6.3 million College of Journalism and Communications building, 'Rae O. Weimer Hall.'" Stephen O'Connell praised Rae in his dedication speech: "It is true that no person should be honored for what he or she has received from life. Honor, such as that bestowed in the naming of this building . . . , ought to be the reward for what one has given to others in living his or her life. By this or any other measure you, Rae Weimer, have earned and richly deserve the honor paid you today." Rae was particularly proud that his son, Rev. Rae O. "Bill" Weimer II, gave both the invocation and benediction at the naming and dedication ceremony.

Weimer Hall may be the country's finest and best-equipped academic journalism building. An atrium with its greenhouse-like roof in the center of the building was designed to reduce heat by 40 percent. Named the Knight Courtyard, it honors the owners and publishers of the *Miami Herald*—in later years they combined to form the Knight-Ridder newspaper chain, at a time one of the nation's largest and most respected newspaper groups. The building may be the only one in the nation with four radio and two television stations under one roof; they include Public Broadcasting Service stations, National Public Radio, a music station, and commercial stations.

36 Final Years

Retirement brought other rewards to Rae as he recounted in a memo for a story about him in the *Communigator* in February 1996: "My principal interest and pleasure now is the frequent contact and visits with former colleagues at the college, university, and my church. Also very important are the visits, letters, and phone calls from former students. The latter is one of the most satisfying things in my life—hearing of former students' successes and activities. [But] the battle with cancer the last four years forced me to give up my volunteer work, and after eighteen years, to forego organizing and leading group tours around the world."

Fortunate to find love and companionship in his final years, Rae married Wilma C. Parvin on May 8, 1993. She supported Rae throughout his battle with prostate cancer from 1992 until he died in 1996. Rae noted that his sixty-three radiation treatments alone "just about killed me. Wilma—she's the one who saved my life. You get all that radiation and you quit eating, but she saw to it that I ate all the right foods."[19] Wilma passed away in 2013 at age ninety-six.

In her "Tribute" to her father at his funeral, his daughter, Ann, described Rae as an extraordinary human being:

> He was the most inquisitive person I've ever known. Some of his queries may have been rhetorical questions or, perhaps, the out-loud musings of a curious mind seeking to learn new things. I did not see him as a deep thinker but someone who had an insatiable curiosity and wanted to learn about his world. He asked about what he saw; he wanted to know what was happening in the world. Both my parents imparted their love of learning—most Christmases my brother and I would find gifts of books under the tree including art books, history books, and all manner of books to treasure and to stimulate our minds. Our house was almost littered with newspapers and magazines piled a foot high on chairs or the coffee table in our living room.

> My dad subscribed to four daily newspapers. Dad was a model father and humanitarian who passed on his values to us. He supported our development with loving, but rational, discipline and admirable standards of conduct.
>
> Equanimity, not emotionality, characterized my father. He and my mother had a very close, supportive and loving relationship. I never heard them argue or disagree in front of us; if they did, it was behind closed doors. My parents were not particularly demonstrative physically, but I always felt loved and supported.
>
> Being fortunate to join Dad's second European tour instilled in me a love of travel that remains today. My father was ever the optimist, a positive person, and one who respected the talents, ideas, and feelings of others. Even when illness or health problems caused him pain and discomfort, he did not give up or become discouraged until the very end. His mind remained sharp as well, such that he impressed many with his wisdom and wealth of historical information. Rae was a truly remarkable man in everything he did and all the roles he played: son, brother, husband, father, newspaperman, journalist, educator, administrator, travel leader, citizen, friend, and human being.

With Rae's death in November 1996 at the age of ninety-three, his beloved family lost a husband, a father, and a grandfather; his community lost a dedicated volunteer and friend; the University of Florida and the State of Florida lost a founding father of journalism. But his legacy lives on even today in one of the nation's largest, most well-equipped, and most acclaimed colleges of journalism and communications in the nation—a college envisioned and brought forth by this self-effacing man of modest beginnings and without a college degree who just wanted to be called "Rae."

37 Legacy

Rae's legacy is more than the tangible building that bears his name; it includes the renowned institution he founded, the service he gave to his community, and the memories of those whose lives he touched.

Innumerable tributes poured in for Weimer's eightieth birthday in 1983. Ben Rowe of the *Independent Farmer & Ranch* wrote: "It would take most of this newspaper to itemize the things Rae O. Weimer has done in his lifetime in service to mankind. He is a shining example of what . . . intelligence was to be made of—common sense. Rae utilized his God-given talents to lead others far better formally educated than he. Without a formal degree, heaven forbid one would ever admit to not owning one of those things now, Weimer elbowed his way into the news business beginning in 1925."[20]

In a piece for the *Florida Newspaper News,* writer Ron Sercombe summed up Weimer's career in Florida with the following: "In 1949 the University of Florida took a gamble on Rae Weimer; the pay-off is still making history." Sercombe further described Weimer as possessing a keen wit, a wonderful sense of humor, and a newspaperman's nose for news: "He likes people . . . as intensely and as understandingly as he dislikes and dismisses red tape. His fondness for people does not extend to stuffed shirts . . . Weimer is a staunch believer in self-discipline and, when warranted, imposed discipline on goof-offs, smart alecks and snobs . . . Folks around Florida often remark, 'They just don't make men like Rae Weimer anymore.'"[21]

Beloved by his faculty, journalism staff member Mickie Newbill once said of Rae: "You are a constant wonder and inspiration to all of us. The sense of dynamism, progression, and comradeship in this school gives us a glow of pride in working here, and it goes without saying that this stems from you. It is my considered opinion that you're the grandest boss I've ever known, and other people on this staff hold you in that same high regard."[22]

Praised for his unselfish service as well as his humility, Rae Weimer garnered numerous honors and awards. Both in their letters nominating Rae for various awards or in presenting him with well-deserved honors, leaders from the community, the university, and around the state penned the following tributes. Many of these tributes came from letters recommending Rae for the Community Service Award in February 1986.

Former University of Florida president Stephen O'Connell wrote in his letter in support of Rae's nomination for the Community Service Award, "There are too few model husbands and fathers, but Rae is one. His character shows through clearly in his every action. He constantly strives to counsel and assist students, faculty, and others with their problems. The numbers indebted to him for wise direction are legion. He is a superb human being." O'Connell admired Rae's "endless enthusiasm, constant optimism, and indefatigable energy."[23]

G. Paul Moore, who knew Rae through the Retired Faculty of the University of Florida, said of him, "To know Rae Weimer as a friend is a privilege. To see his constant, unselfish, and extensive contributions to the local and larger communities is a great inspiration . . . Perhaps, the most remarkable feature of his service is the quiet, unobtrusive, selfless manner in which he provides it."[24]

One of the University of Florida College of Journalism and Communications' professors that Rae hired, Dr. Glenn Butler, noted, "Dr. Weimer is a modest person and does not seek recognition. He only seeks to serve others."[25]

"The best thing Rae Weimer has done for the Gainesville and university communities is to share himself with people of all ages and walks of life," said Director of Information and Publications Linda Gray. "Young people are continuously amazed at the energy and dynamic personality reflected by a man over eighty. He also truly listens when others speak and speaks the truth himself."[26]

In another of the many February 1986 letters recommending Rae for the Community Service Award, D. R. "Billy" Matthews posited that "no civilization can survive unless it produces enough citizens who give more to that civilization than they take away. This service must be ecumenical—to the elite and to the poor. I know of no person in our community who can surpass this concept of good citizenship that I perceive in my friend, Rae Weimer."[27]

Weimer's successor as dean of the University of Florida College of Journalism and Communications, John Paul Jones, acknowledged Rae's leadership qualities: "He was a tremendous person to work with—probably the most understanding and humane person I ever worked with. He was able to obtain a lot of work from his faculty because he set the example. He was on the job all the time. This was contagious. This is the way you build a great institution. He gave you complete freedom to do what you wanted to do as long as you did it. Weimer is the first to call on you when you're ill, and the first to give praise when you earn it. But when necessary, he'll demand more effort from you. He doesn't just hire you, stick you in a corner, and forget you. He respects your opinion, constantly asks for assistance and advice, and seeks to implement your ideas.[28]

Family values were important to Rae. Pulitzer Prize–winning journalist H. G. "Buddy" Davis explained his attraction to the University of Florida College of Journalism and Communications as well as his impression of Rae as a family man: "Another talent which Rae amply demonstrated was human relations—and not just with the Florida press and others of every possible political persuasion. Permit one small example. My wife and I contracted to build a house in 1967, and Rae insisted, somewhat foolishly I thought, on visiting the site. We met him and Ruth there, under a roof supported by a few bricks and sticks, with this spot going to be the living room and this spot a den and this spot a bath. At that point, from a paper bag, Rae whipped out a bottle of champagne and four plastic goblets for a toast to our good fortune. Now I ask you, to a boss like that, would you give a hard time? Long before 'family values' exploded into political rhetoric, long before the term 'nuclear family' crept into sociology textbooks, Rae Weimer was a family man—stable, caring, protective, loving. Over the many years that I observed, it was amply demonstrated with his wife Ruth and his upbringing of two eminently successful children, Ann and Bill."[29]

Dean emeritus of the University of Florida College of Journalism and Communications Ralph L. Lowenstein praised Rae's contribution to the college: "Rae Weimer founded the college on two principles. One, this would be a professional school, based strongly on solid, hands-on training for the media professions. Second, this would be a school for all communications media—journalism, advertising, broadcasting, and public relations, without any apologies for the teaching of any of those professions. Rae Weimer's legacy is that those principles permeate the life of the college today"[30]

Bruce Morris, a journalism graduate, summed up his impression of Rae in his piece "It's the Magnetism Within": "Rae Weimer has been in every state of the union except three and nearly all over the world. But, basically, he's just a small-town boy. His friendships transcend all boundaries . . . He may not possess vast fame and fortune. But, if you measure wealth in terms of friends, respect, and prestige, then Rae O. Weimer is a very rich man."[31]

Patricia Wilkinson, an editor for the *Gainesville Sun*, bemoaned Weimer's leaving his post as dean, writing: "For the man's genius in getting along with and understanding people, pervades the halls, classrooms, and offices. No rudeness, shortness, or indifference there. Everyone is a very important person to be treated with courtesy and unusual consideration. Mr. Weimer drives himself and everyone around him and they like it."[32]

A friend since *PM* days, Max Lerner, wrote him a congratulatory letter on May 9, 1968, for Rae's retirement, which read: "The occasion of your retiring as dean spurs many memories in me, all of them nostalgic and all of them good. I was a lucky young columnist, in the days of *PM*, to have a managing editor like Rae Weimer to work under. In terms of newspaper experience I was still wet behind the ears, and you gave me a good drying. I was callow at in-fighting, and you taught me the ropes. I was still green from the Ivy League college teaching posts and you taught me what a good newspaper man does, and is. I shall never forget those years, nor your role in them, nor the warmth of our friendship and fellowship. What I learned from you and working with you, spilled over into all the rest of my life. You will never actually retire because no good newspaper man ever stops being one until the day his breath stops."[33]

Former students shared their thoughts about the retiring dean in the May 1968 special issue of the *Florida Press* entitled "Dean Rae O. Weimer—A Tribute." Here are some of their comments:

His personality is his biggest asset.

He's a very warm person. He's interested in the problems of students.

I have never heard a derogatory remark against him.

> I feel Dean Weimer's resignation will be the greatest loss the College of Journalism has ever suffered. He has built this college and he is the college. More importantly, he is one of the nicest and most generous men I know.

The unknown author who compiled the student comments remarked: "His office door is wide open for anyone who wants to walk in to talk with him. And that little twinkle in his eyes lets a student know that he understands their problems. Dean Weimer has brought the note of prestige to the college. His name is generally recognized as being one of the outstanding administrators and educators around the country. His name is known far and wide, and so is his school."[34]

In that same *Florida Press* issue, another unknown author told the story of Rae's obtaining much needed photographic equipment early on: "The progress-minded Weimer asked for and was promptly denied permission to obtain photographic equipment for his school. Seeing that the students' needs were of greater importance than the risk he was taking, Weimer had the equipment purchased and placed in an inconspicuous corner of the journalism building." After using the equipment, students would cover it with camouflage. Upon discovering the equipment during an inspection, "the inspector went into a mildly heated rage: 'What's this? You're not allowed to have this equipment!' Today, [1968] . . . the College of Journalism and Communications has one of the largest and most productive photojournalism departments in the nation." Without Weimer's ability to see the need and to risk "denunciation or even expulsion," none of this would have happened.[35]

Rae Weimer credited others for much of the success of journalism at the University of Florida. "Just think about all the people who were involved with making that school a success. I sometimes think the head man gets more credit than he deserves. I didn't build it alone; many people worked awfully hard without receiving the credit due them. I couldn't have built the School into a College without tremendous help."[36]

Stephen O'Connell, in his speech at the dedication of Weimer Hall, had this to say: "I doubt that Ruth and Rae acquired much in the material things that could have been theirs had they chosen to continue in the private side of their profession. They simply did not mistake the material pleasures of life for happiness, nor measure success by wealth acquired. Rather, they chose to give their lives building for the benefit of others, to serve this university, to counsel, to encourage, to lead, and to inspire the students and faculty of this college. And in so doing they have amassed a veritable fortune in that golden currency, which is counted in the reflected love, affection, respect, admiration, and gratitude held for them by the many whose hearts have been warmed, intellects sharpened and expanded, and lives bettered by the cheerful, unselfish actions of the Weimers."[37]

Rae's legacy also lives on through two scholarships established through private gifts in Rae's (and Ruth's) name at the University of Florida College of Journalism and Communications. The top College awards are the Weimer Awards, named for Rae O. Weimer and his wife Ruth. The Ruth and Rae O. Weimer Scholarship Fund provides job-hunting support for the outstanding graduate student at the time of graduation. In 2022, the endowment value of this scholarship fund was $25,763, generating about $950 each year. There were originally 147 donors to this fund. Another fund is the Rae O. Weimer Scholarship Fund for Undergraduates. This fund in 2022 had an endowment value of $226,717, generating about $8,250 each year to benefit usually two to three students. There were originally more than 240 donors who gave $124,115 in gifts.[38]

The legacy of this journalism founding father without a college degree continues today. Of finally receiving his honorary degree, Rae recalled, "Many stories in the press mentioned that this was my first degree. If one counted from the year I first enrolled in college, it was fifty-two years later that I received my first degree. And the university seldom gives a degree to one of their own; usually it is someone from outside. It really was something special. The headline in the story in the university's magazine read, 'Now You Can Call Him Dr. Weimer.'" No longer auburn-haired, silver-haired Rae added, "I just hope nobody stops calling me Rae."

Afterword

Both Rae's children graduated from the University of Florida. His son, Bill, graduated in April 1967 from the College of Journalism and Communications founded by his father. Then, it was off to the Navy's Officer Candidate School in Newport, Rhode Island, where he was commissioned as an ensign that July. Just prior to his first deployment with the Sixth Fleet in the Mediterranean, Bill married Eathel Bowie at her home in Anderson, South Carolina. They had two boys, Hunter in 1971, and Ryan in 1974, both of whom had the good fortune to know their grandfather, Rae Weimer. After retiring from the Navy, Bill and Eathel moved to Mariner Sands in Stuart, Florida, where Bill served as a pastor for eight years. The Weimers now reside at a retirement community in Atlantic Beach, Florida.

Rae's daughter-in-law, Eathel Weimer, appreciated Rae's openness and insistence on honesty in relationships as she related the following anecdote: "Dad taught me that being honest was more important to him than being polite. My southern heritage emphasized politeness over honesty. One Christmas, I saw that they [Rae and Ruth] had bought their grandson a Tonka toy tractor, which he already had. So, trying to 'be polite,' I hid the one we already had in what I thought was a safe hiding place. Dad, being the curious man that he was, found [the toy] hidden in a space under our house while he was checking out our home's foundation. He confronted me by saying, 'Eathel, there is no need to hide the truth from me. We can deal with the truth together.' What a great life lesson. He and Mother [Ruth] were truly a gift to me and my family."

One of Rae's grandsons, Ryan, was particularly fond of visiting his grandfather and shared his sentiments, "He was a loving and loyal grandparent, calling us each Sunday evening. He was a natural leader, with keen interpersonal skills. I remember him as an optimistic, positive person who wanted to be productive and solve problems, often with a diverse group of people. One spring break during my high school years (probably around 1990), I spent a week with him. By the end, I was worn out! Each day, he planned on me tagging along to several of his meetings with the College of Journalism, hospital board, Kiwanis Club, and other civic organizations. His energy and charm were infectious. He even set up an informational meeting for me with Mr. Edward Peddie, president and CEO of Alachua General Hospital/Santa Fe [Health Care]. He also organized a lunch for me at the Sigma Chi house. Each day was well thought-out, and informative for me as I thought about different schools and vocations."

Rae's daughter, Ann, also graduated from the University of Florida. Majoring in psychology she received a bachelor of arts degree with high honors, a master of science degree in psychology, and a PhD in clinical psychology. Ann later completed a postdoctorate degree in neuropsychology at the San Francisco VA Medical Center. Her entire career was spent in service to those with disabilities, first at Monroe Developmental Center in Rochester, New York, and then at the California School for the Deaf in Fremont, California. Ann and her second husband, James Solar, live in a retirement community in Fairfield, California.

On a visit to see his brother, Rae, in Gainesville, Doc was invited to join the *St. Petersburg Times,* run by Nelson Poynter. Doc and Poynter had worked together at the *Columbus Citizen.* In March 1952, Doc and Lillian Weimer and their children as well as Rae's and Doc's parents moved to Treasure Island in the St. Petersburg area. Doc continued his career in public relations with the *Times* in the capacity of associate publisher for two years. He also commuted to Columbus, Ohio, to manage the Weimer Organization and to oversee his own newspaper, the *Daily Sentinel* in Pomeroy, Ohio. Due to a congenital heart defect, Doc underwent delicate heart surgery in Philadelphia with a successful outcome but succumbed to complications a week later in July 1955. He was fifty-three years old. A humble man who spurned attention to his accomplishments, Claud F. "Doc" Weimer was held in high regard by his peers and by the civic and business groups he served, especially in Ohio and Florida. Rae's mother and father continued to live in Treasure Island until their deaths in 1964 and 1965 at ages eighty-five and eighty-nine, respectively.

Appendix I

Professional Experience

Newspaper Experience

The Antelope, Kearney, NE, 1922–25, Editor (College newspaper)

North Platte Herald, North Platte, NE, 1925, News Editor

Paragould Daily Press, Paragould, AR, 1925, Editor

Moline Dispatch, Moline, IL, 1925, Reporter

Marion Star, Marion, OH, 1925–26, Reporter–State Editor

Olean Herald, Olean, NY, 1926–27, Sports Editor and Telegraph Editor

Journal Gazette, Fort Wayne, IN, 1927–28, State Editor

Indianapolis Times, Indianapolis, IN, 1928, Copy Desk

Beacon Journal, Akron, OH, 1928–30, State Editor; 1931–1933, Assistant City Editor

Akron Times-Press, Akron, OH, 1934–35, Assistant City Editor; 1936–37, News Editor

Buffalo Times, Buffalo, NY, 1938–39, Assistant City Editor

Cleveland Press, Cleveland, OH, 1939–1940, Copy Reader

PM, New York, NY, 1940–46, Assistant Managing Editor; 1946–48, Managing Editor

Other Experience

The Weimer Organization (Public Relations), Columbus, OH, 1948–49, Vice President; 1956–57, President

School of Journalism and Communications, University of Florida, Gainesville, FL, 1949–67, Founder and Director

WUFT Public Broadcasting Station, Gainesville, FL, 1955–57, Founder and Station Manager

College of Journalism and Communications, University of Florida, Gainesville, FL, 1967–68, Dean; 1973–74, Dean Emeritus and Director of Development

University of Florida, Gainesville, FL, 1968–73, Special Assistant to the President

Ruth Weimer's Experience

Bachelor of Arts from the University of Oklahoma, 1931

Reporter, Assistant Society Editor of the *Oklahoma City Times*, 1932–34

Society Editor of the *Oklahoma City Times*, 1934–37

Assistant Women's Editor of the *Akron Times-Press*, 1937–38

Society Editor and Assistant Women's Editor for the *Oklahoma City Times* and *Oklahoman*, 1938–1942

Columnist, Women's Editor of the *Gainesville Sun*, 1950–55; 1962–66

Appendix II

Honors and Awards

1962: Citation for Outstanding Service to the State of Florida from Governor Farris Bryant

1965: Honorary Member of Florida Blue Key

1965: State Press Award for Outstanding Service to Journalism in Florida

1967: Honorary Membership in the Florida Press Association

1968: Honorary Membership in the Alumni Association of the University of Florida

1968: Distinguished Service Award from the University of Florida Chapter of the Public Relations Student Society of America

1968: Aid to Advertising Education Award from Alpha Delta Sigma (one of five awarded nationally)

1970: Honorary member of Omicron Delta Kappa

1970: Honorary member of Alpha Phi Gamma, journalism honorary

1974: University of Florida Citation from President Robert Marston

1974: Honorary Doctor of Letters

1980: Outstanding Alumni Awards, Kearney State College

1980: Florida Department of Agriculture and Consumer Services Award

1981: Naming of the University of Florida's College of Journalism and Communications building: "Rae O. Weimer Hall" by special action of the Florida Legislature

1985: *Gainesville Sun* Community Service Award

1987: Paul Harris Fellow from the Rotary Club of Gainesville for "furtherance of better understanding and relations among people of the world"

1989: E. T. York Service Above Self Award from the Rotary Club of Gainesville for "his outstanding, dedicated, unselfish service which has enhanced the personal quality of the lives of local citizens"

1990: Inducted into the Florida Newspaper Hall of Fame

1992: University of Florida Presidential Medallion presented by University President John V. Lombardi to Dean Emeritus Rae O. Weimer

Appendix III

Weimer Tours

1942: Cuba

1947: Iceland

1950: Cuba

1956: Europe (also in 1961, 1963, 1965, 1980)

1967: Scandinavia

1969: Greece, Turkey, and Mediterranean Islands

1970: England and Scotland

1971: Adriatic Cruise

1973: Balkans

1975: Orient

1976: Australia, New Zealand, and South Pacific Islands

1977: South America

1977: Mexico

1978: Middle East

1978: Guatemala

1979: Alaska

1980: Mainland China

1981: Bermuda

1981: Kenya

1981: Italy

1983: Costa Rica

1984: South Africa

1987: Italy

Notes

Part I. Native Nebraskan

1. "Welcome to Custer County Nebraska," Custer County, Nebraska, accessed June 6, 2022, https://custercountyne.gov/webpages/about/history.html.

2. Bill Ganzel, "Rise and Fall of the Omaha Stockyards," *Ganzel Group*, https://livinghistoryfarm.org/farming-in-the-1950s/making-money/the-rise-fall-of-the-omaha-stockyards/.

3. Carolyn Dimitri, Anne Effland, and Neilson Conklin, "The 20th Century Transformation of U.S. Agriculture and Farm Policy." *USDA Economic Information Bulletin,* no. 3 (June 2005).

4. Various organizations such as the Grange, the Farmers' Alliance, and Chautauqua provided rural residents exposure to the arts as well as educational programs. The Circuit Chautauqua was a traveling group of performers who provided entertainment and culture including inspirational speakers, lecturers, musicians, and showmen to rural America. Other innovations of the times that eased the isolation of rural life were movies and radio.

5. Thomas A. Kirwan, "Rae O. Weimer: Pioneer of Journalism Education in Florida," Master's thesis, University of Florida, 1986.

6. Kirwan, 5.

7. Lauren Sedam, "Wagon Reveals Part of History of Horse, Mule Markets." *Grand Island Independent*, January 6, 2016; updated September 24, 2019, https://theindependent.com/news/local/wagon-reveals-part-of-history-of-horse-mule-markets.

8. Ron Sercombe, "Florida's Most Dynamic Dean." *Florida Newspaper News and Radio Digest,* 49, no. 6 (July 1968): 4.

9. Kirwan, 5.

10. Kirwan, 9.

11. *The Perils of Pauline* was a 1914 melodramatic film serial produced by William Randolph Hearst in twenty- to thirty-minute biweekly installments shown through the 1920s.

12. The Civil War–reconstruction epic, *Birth of a Nation*, was a landmark 1914 silent film proclaimed for its use of special effects. It was the first Hollywood blockbuster as well as the longest (nearly three hours) and most profitable film at that time. Due to its racist portrayal of Blacks, there were protests at the

premiere. The film also resurrected a moribund Ku Klux Klan following the film's debut in Atlanta.

13. Kirwan, 10.

14. Kirwan, 13.

15. Rae Weimer, personal notes from a speech given at Kearney State College, October 15, 1985, quoted in Kirwan, 14.

16. Kirwan, 15.

17. Bruce A. Morris, "It's the Magnetism Within," Unknown publication (n.d.), 4.

18. Kirwan, 18.

Part II. A Plethora of Papers

1. Horance G. Davis, "An Editorial," *Communigator*, January 1968, 16.

2. Kirwan, 18.

3. Because Thorpe had played semipro sports before the Olympics, he lost his two gold medals—one for the decathlon and one for the pentathlon. It was not until thirty years later in 1983 that his medals were restored to his family.

4. History.com Editors, "Professional Football Is Born," November 16, 2009, https://www.history.com/this-day-in-history/professional-football-is-born.

5. "Marion Steam Shovel Company," Ohio History Central, accessed February 5, 2022, https://ohiohistorycentral.org/w/Marion_Steam_Shovel_Company.

6. Kirwan, 28.

7. Justin Clark, "The Indianapolis Times: A Short History," *Hoosier State Chronicles*, April 13, 2017, https://blog.newspapers.library.in.gov/indianapolis-times.

8. "Indianapolis Times Pulitzer Prize–Winning Daily Newspaper Published from 1888 to 1965," IUPUI: The Polis Center, accessed November 21, 2022, https://polis.iupui.edu/indianapolis-times-pulitzer-prize-winning-daily-newspaper-published-from-1888-to-1965.

9. Richard K. Smith, *The Airships Akron & Macon: Flying Aircraft Carriers of the United States Navy* (Annapolis, MD: Naval Institute Press, 1965), 162.

10. *Florida Press*, "Rae and Ruth Weimer: A Newsroom Courtship," May 1968, 7.

Part III. *PM*—A Pioneer Publication

1. Lewis Donohew, "*PM:* An Anniversary Assessment," *Columbia Journalism Review*, Summer 1965, 33.

2. Kirwan, 38.

3. Roy Hoopes, "Ingersoll, Poynter Collaborated on *PM*," *St. Petersburg Times*, March 17, 1985.

4. Kirwan, 41.

5. Kirwan, 40

6. Bruce Morris, "It's the Magnetism Within," 6.

7. *PM*, "Prospectus to Sell 100,000 More *PMs* a Day," June 18, 1946.

8. Milkman, Paul, *PM: A New Deal in Journalism 1940–1948* (Denver: Outskirts Press, 2016), 18.

9. Kirwan, 47.

10. John Simkin, "*PM* Newspaper," *Spartacus Educational*, September 1997; updated January 2020, https://spartacus-educational.com/PMnew.htm.

11. Milkman, 94.

12. Lisa Barr, *Iguana*, January 1993, 2.

13. Myra MacPherson, *All Governments Lie! The Life and Times of Rebel Journalist I. F. Stone* (New York: A Lisa Drew Book/Scribner, 2006), 206.

14. MacPherson, 115.

15. MacPherson, 206.

16. Max Lerner to Rae Weimer, May 9, 1968, "Memories of Max Lerner," *Florida Press*, May 1968, 5.

17. Morris, 6.

18. David Margolick, "*PM*'s Impossible Dream," *Vanity Fair*, January 1999, 120.

19. Personal papers in the estate of Rae Weimer.

20. "Margaret Bourke-White: Biography & Legacy," The Art Story, accessed December 20, 2021, https://www.theartstory.org/artist/bourke-white-margaret/life-and-legacy.

21. Ralph Ingersoll, Memorandum to the Staff, March 24, 1942, personal files of Rae Weimer.

22. Lisa Barr, *Iguana*, January 1993, 2.

23. Ingersoll, Memorandum to the Editorial Board, June 6, 1941, personal files of Rae Weimer.

24. Ingersoll, Memorandum to the Staff, January 13, 1941, personal files of Rae Weimer.

25. Rae Weimer interviewed in 1994 by Paul Milkman for *PM: A New Deal in Journalism 1940–1948*, personal files of Rae Weimer.

26. Personal files of Rae Weimer.

27. Ingersoll, Memorandum to the Staff, June 18, 1941, personal files of Rae Weimer.

28. Francis S. Wickware, "Marshall Field III: He Tries to Atone for His Many Millions by Good Works and Profitless Journalism," *Life*, October 18, 1943, 103.

29. I. F. Stone, "The Meaning of the Associated Press Ruling," *PM*, June 20, 1945.

30. Kirwan, 42. Printers typed letters on a wide keyboard, before molten lead would be pressed against a mat with the typed letters. This lead hardened into a "slug" that then fell into a metal tray—or "galley"—used to print preliminary pages of type, or "proofs" to be proofread and edited as needed before being sent back to the printer—a time-consuming process.

31. Donohew, 35.

32. Morris, 3.

33. Rae Weimer interviewed by Paul Milkman, 1994, personal files of Rae Weimer.

34. Ingersoll, Memorandum to the staff, January 7, 1942; Talk to the Staff, January 5, 1942, personal files of Rae Weimer.

35. John Lewis, Memorandum to staff of *PM,* November 25, 1942, personal files of Rae Weimer.

36. Lewis, Private document in estate of Rae O. Weimer.

37. Morris, 7.

38. MacPherson, 206.

39. Milkman, 167.

40. Milkman, 167.

41. Milkman, 105.

42. Donohew, 36.

43. Davis, "An Editorial."

44. *Florida Press,* "A Newsroom Courtship."

45. Margaret T. Shonbrun, "On Rae Weimer, *PM,* and a Steamer Up the Hudson River to Bear Mountain," *Gainesville Sun,* July 19, 1983.

46. John L. Lewis, "Copy Boy," *PM,* April 3, 1944, 14.

47. Gerald Blank, "How the Tenants of an Apartment House Started a Co-operative Nursery School," *PM,* February 13, 1947, 12–13.

48. Milkman, 347.

49. Milkman, 377.

50. Milkman, 378.

51. Milkman, 391–92.

52. Personal files of Rae Weimer.

53. Roy Hoopes, "When Ingersoll Papered Manhattan," *Washington Journalism Review,* December 1984, 32.

54. Margolick, 121.

55. John Lewis to F. W. McDonough, editor, *Better Homes and Gardens,* April 27, 1948.

Part IV. University of Florida

1. Davidson was later inducted into the Florida Newspaper Hall of Fame in 1989. Its brochure of inductees noted that he "fought tirelessly on behalf of open government, civil rights, and the First Amendment" including a role in the 1934 Florida Supreme Court decision affirming the public's right to inspect records.

2. Judy Hamilton, "The Mythmakers Don't Have Rae Weimer Anymore," *Florida Accent,* October 13, 1974, 6.

3. Morris, 6, 8.

4. Sercombe, "Florida's Most Dynamic Dean."

5. Hamilton, "Mythmakers Don't Have Rae," 6.

6. Tad Wegman, "Dean Emeritus Weimer Misses Students at Journalism School," *Gainesville Sun,* May 2, 1977, front page.

7. Hamilton, "Mythmakers Don't Have Rae," 6.

8. Al Azula, "A College Traces Its Roots," *Communigator,* Fall 1968, 9.

9. Hamilton, "Mythmakers Don't Have Rae," 6.

10. Jim Tunstall, "The Father of Florida Journalism," *Tampa Tribune,* August 17, 1994.

11. Kirwan, 59.

12. John Paul Jones, "A Brief History: 1926–1976," *Communigator,* Winter 1976, https://www.jou.ufl.edu/cjc-history-062119/history-of-the-college.

13. Rae Weimer interview by Samuel Proctor, 1969, transcript of oral history interview November 4, 1974, personal files of Rae Weimer.

14. Rae Weimer interview by Samuel Proctor, 111.

15. Rae Weimer interview by Samuel Proctor, 140.

16. *St. Petersburg Times* Editorial, "Journalism Could Lead in New Educational Finance Methods," 1959.

17. *Florida Press,* "Personal Concern Built UF Faculty," May 1968, 15.

18. Morris, 9.

19. Azula, "A College Traces Its Roots," 9.

20. Sercombe, "Florida's Most Dynamic Dean."

21. *St. Petersburg Times,* "Journalism Could Lead."

22. *Florida Press,* "UF First in Hearst Again!" May 1968, 7.

23. Horance G. Davis, "Weimer Appointed Dean; Announces Step-Down," *Communigator*, January 1, 1968, 1.

24. Jones, "A Brief History."

25. Hugh W. Cunningham, "Retired Faculty Comments about Rae Weimer," *Communigator*, Spring 1997.

26. Hugh W. Cunningham, "Latest Hearst Award Brings Total to Eight," *Communigator*, January 1, 1968, 1.

27. Azula, "A College Traces Its Roots."

28. Sydney Foster, "The Top 10 Journalism Schools 2019," *College Magazine*, April 4, 2019, updated May 12, 2022, http://collegemagazine.com/top-journalism-schools-2019.

29. "2023 Best Colleges for Communications in America," *Niche*, accessed December 4, 2022, https://www.niche.com/colleges/search/best-colleges-for-communications.

30. "Journalism at University of Florida," *College Factual*, accessed January 29, 2022, https://www.collegefactual.com/colleges/university-of-florida/academic-life/academic-majors/communication-journalism-media/journalism.

31. Francesca Fulciniti, "The 12 Best Journalism Schools," *PrepScholar*, August 20, 2021, https://blog.prepscholar.com/best-journalism-schools.

32. "20 Best Journalism Schools (Bachelor's) 2022," *College Rank*, https://www.collegerank.net/best-bachelors-journalism.

33. "Discover the 10 Best Colleges for Journalism in the US," *College Gazette*, September 20, 2019, https://collegegazette.com/discover-the-10-best-colleges-for-journalism-in-the-us.

34. Proctor, Interview of Rae Weimer, 143.

35. Jim Moorehead, "Weimer Scholars," *Communigator,* Fall 1994, 18–19.

36. Stephen O'Connell, "Dedication of Weimer Hall," October 24, 1981, personal files of Rae Weimer.

37. Stephen O'Connell, "Dedication of Weimer Hall."

Part V. Seeing the World

1. Bill Adams, "Weimer's Bag Packed with Travel Experience," *Florida Business Journal,* November 25, 1965, 1.

2. Adams, 1.

3. Adams, 1.

4. Hugh W. Cunningham to Community Service Award, January 24, 1986, personal files of Rae Weimer.

5. Adams, "Weimer's Bag Packed."

Part VI. Retirement Years

1. Julie Stricker, "Busier Than Ever, Rae Weimer Recognized with Rotary Award," *Gainesville Sun,* January 11, 1989, 1D.

2. Cunningham to Community Service Award.

3. Leveda Brown quoted in Cunningham to Community Service Award.

4. Tad Wegman, "Dean Misses Students," *Gainesville Sun,* May 2, 1977.

5. Horace G. Davis to Dr. Wayne H. Chen, dean of the College of Engineering, University of Florida, March 13, 1974, personal files of Rae Weimer.

6. Paul Jones, Presentation at Award Ceremony, 1968, personal files of Rae Weimer.

7. Robert Marston, Conferring of Honorary Degree, 1968, personal files of Rae Weimer.

8. Bruce Dudley, "J-School's Weimer Honored," *Florida Alligator* (n.d.).

9. Gainesville Rotary Club, "Service Above Self Award" brochure, January 10, 1989.

10. Randy Caton quoted in Stricker, "Busier Than Ever."

11. Ross Mackenzie quoted in Cunningham to Community Service Award.

12. Jones, "A Brief History."

13. *Florida Alligator,* "Journalism Building to Be Named for Weimer in Saturday Ceremony," October 21, 1981.

14. *Florida Alligator,* "Journalism Building to Be Named for Weimer in Saturday Ceremony."

15. Cunningham to Community Service Award.

16. Jeff Hardison, "New Name for Journalism Building Honors Former Dean," *Gainesville Sun*, October 22, 1981.

17. O'Connell, "Dedication of Weimer Hall."

18. Hardison, "New Name for Building."

19. Jim Tunstall, "The Father of Florida Journalism," *Tampa Tribune,* August 17, 1994, 5.

20. J. Ben Rowe, "Happy Birthday Rae O. Weimer," *Independent Farmer & Ranch,* November 3, 1983.

21. Sercombe, "Florida's Most Dynamic Dean."

22. Mickie Newbill, Memo to Mr. Rae O. Weimer, June 13, 1957, personal files of Rae Weimer.

23. Stephen O'Connell to Community Service Award, February 12, 1986, personal files of Rae Weimer.

24. G. Paul Moore to Community Service Award, February 6, 1986, personal files of Rae Weimer.

25. Glenn Butler to Community Service Award, February 12, 1986, personal files of Rae Weimer.

26. Linda Gray to Community Service Award, February 4, 1986, personal files of Rae Weimer.

27. D. R. (Billy) Matthews to Community Service Award, February 8, 1986, personal files of Rae Weimer.

28. Paul Jones quoted in Morris, "It's the Magnetism Within," 9.

29. Horace G. Davis, "A Man with Talent for Human Relations," *Communigator,* Spring 1997, 11.

30. Ralph Lowenstein, Comments about Rae Weimer, *Communigator,* Spring 1997, 11.

31. Morris, "It's the Magnetism Within," 9.

32. Patricia Wilkinson, "Mr. Weimer Appreciated," *Gainesville Sun* (n.d.).

33. Max Lerner to Rae Weimer.

34. *Florida Press,* "Person-to-Person Counseling Aids Both Students and Profs," May 1968, 8.

35. *Florida Press,* "An Action-Minded Successor?" May 1968, 19.

36. Stricker, "Busier Than Ever."

37. O'Connell, "Dedication of Weimer Hall."

38. "Annual Endowment Report," UF Donor Relations to Ann Weimer Moxley (email), November 14, 2022.

Bibliography

Adams, Bill. "Weimer's Bag Packed with Travel Experience." *Florida Business Journal,* November 25, 1965.

"Annual Endowment Report." UF Donor Relations to Ann Weimer Moxley (email), November 14, 2022.

The Art Story. "Margaret Bourke-White: Biography & Legacy." https://www.theartstory.org/artist/bourke-white-margaret/life-and-legacy (accessed December 20, 2021).

Azula, Al. "A College Traces Its Roots . . ." *Communigator,* Fall 1968, 9.

Barr, Lisa. *Iguana,* January 1993.

Blank, Gerald. "How the Tenants of an Apartment House Started a Co-operative Nursery School." *PM,* February 13, 1947, 12–13.

Brown, Leveda. Quoted in Cunningham to Community Service Award. January 24, 1986.

Butler, Glenn. Community Service Award, February 12, 1986, personal files of Rae Weimer.

Caton, Randy. Quoted in Stricker, "Busier Than Ever." January 11, 1989.

Clark, Justin. "The Indianapolis Times: A Short History." *Hoosier State Chronicles:* Indiana's Digital Historic Newspaper Program, April 13, 2017. https://blog.newspapers.library.in.gov/indianapolis-times.

College Factual. "Journalism at University of Florida." https://www.collegefactual.com/colleges/university-of-florida/academic-life/academic-majors/communication-journalism-media/journalism/ (accessed January 29, 2022).

College Gazette. "Discover the 10 Best Colleges for Journalism in the US." September 30, 2019. https://collegegazette.com/discover-the-10-best-colleges-for-journalism-in-the-us.

College Rank. "20 Best Journalism Schools (Bachelor's) 2022." https://www.collegerank.net/best-bachelors-journalism/ (accessed November 21, 2022).

Cunningham, Hugh W. "Latest Hearst Award Brings Total to Eight." *Communigator,* 18, no. 1, January 1, 1968.

Cunningham, Hugh W., to the Community Service Award, January 24, 1986, personal files of Rae Weimer.

Cunningham, Hugh W. "Retired Faculty Comments about Rae Weimer." *Communigator,* Spring 1997.

Custer County, Nebraska. "Welcome to Custer County Nebraska." 2014. https://custercountyne.gov/webpages/about/history.html.

Davis, Horance G. "Weimer Appointed Dean; Announces 'Step-down.'" *Communigator,* 18, no. 1, January 1968.

Davis, Horance G. "An Editorial." *Communigator,* January 1968.

Davis, Horance G. to Dr. Wayne H. Chen, Dean of the College of Engineering, University of Florida, March 13, 1974, personal files of Rae Weimer.

Davis, Horance G. "A Man with Talent for Human Relations." *Communigator,* Spring 1997, 11.

Dimitri, Carolyn, Anne Effland, and Neilson Conklin. "The 20th Century Transformation of U.S. Agriculture and Farm Policy." *USDA Economic Information Bulletin No. 3* (June 2005). https://www.ers.usda.gov/webdocs/publications/44197/13566_eib3_1_.pdf.

Donohew, Lewis. "*PM:* An Anniversary Assessment." *Columbia Journalism Review,* Summer 1965, 33–36.

Dudley, Bruce. "J-School's Weimer Honored." *Florida Alligator* (n.d.).

Florida Alligator. "Journalism Building to Be Named for Weimer in Saturday Ceremony." October 21, 1981.

Florida Press. "Rae and Ruth Weimer: A Newsroom Courtship." May 1968.

Florida Press. "An Action-Minded Successor?" May 1968.

Florida Press. "Person-to-Person Counseling Aids Both Students and Profs." May 1968, 8.

Florida Press. "Personal Concern Built UF Faculty." May 1968, 15.

Florida Press. "UF First in Hearst Again!" May 1968, 7.

Foster, Sydney. "The Top 10 Journalism Schools 2019." *College Magazine,* April 4, 2019; updated May 12, 2022, http://collegemagazine.com/top-journalism-schools-2019.

Fulciniti, Francesca. "The 12 Best Journalism Schools." *PrepScholar,* August 20, 2021. https://blog.prepscholar.com/best-journalism-schools.

Gainesville Rotary Club. "Service Above Self Award." Brochure, January 10, 1989.

Gainesville Sun. "Rae O. Weimer." November 16, 1996, Editorial Page.

Ganzel, Bill. "Rise and Fall of the Omaha Stockyards." *Ganzel Group,* 2007. https://livinghistoryfarm.org/farming-in-the-1950s/making-money/the-rise-fall-of-the-omaha-stockyards/.

Gray, Linda. Community Service Award, February 4, 1986, personal files of Rae Weimer.

Hamilton, Judy. "The Mythmakers Don't Have Rae Weimer Anymore." *Florida Accent,* October 13, 1974, 6.

Hardison, Jeff. "New Name for Journalism Building Honors Former Dean." *Gainesville Sun,* October 22, 1981.

History.com Editors. "Professional Football Is Born." November 16, 2009. https://www.history.com/this-day-in-history/professional-football-is-born.
Hoopes, Roy. "When Ralph Ingersoll Papered Manhattan." *Washington Journalism Review,* December 1984, 25–32.
Hoopes, Roy. "Ingersoll, Poynter Collaborated on *PM.*" *St. Petersburg Times,* March 17, 1985.
Ingersoll, Ralph. Memorandum to the Staff, January 13, 1941, personal files of Rae Weimer.
Ingersoll, Ralph. Memorandum to the Editorial Board, June 6, 1941, personal files of Rae Weimer.
Ingersoll, Ralph. Memorandum to the Staff, June 18, 1941, personal files of Rae Weimer.
Ingersoll, Ralph. Talk to Staff, January 5, 1942, personal files of Rae Weimer.
Ingersoll, Ralph. Memo to the Staff, January 7, 1942, personal files of Rae Weimer.
Ingersoll, Ralph. Memo to the Staff, March 24, 1942, personal files of Rae Weimer.
Ingersoll, Ralph. "Letter to Marshall Field, October 31, 1946," *PM,* November 5, 1946.
IUPUI: The Polis Center. "Indianapolis Times Pulitzer Prize–Winning Daily Newspaper Published from 1888 to 1965." https://polis.iupui.edu/indianapolis-times-pulitzer-prize-winning-daily-newspaper-published-from-1888-to-1965/ (accessed November 21, 2022).
Jones, John Paul. Presentation at Award Ceremony, 1968, personal files of Rae Weimer.
Jones, John Paul. "A Brief History: 1926–1976." *Communigator,* Winter 1976. https://www.jou.ufl.edu/cjc-history-062119/history-of-the-college/.
Kirwan, Thomas A. "Rae O. Weimer: Pioneer of Journalism Education in Florida." Master's thesis, University of Florida, 1986.
Lerner, Max. "Farwell and Hail." *PM,* April 29, 1948.
Lerner, Max. "Memories of Max Lerner." *Florida Press,* May 9, 1968, 5.
Lewis, John L. Memorandum to staff of *PM,* November 25, 1942, personal files of Rae Weimer.
Lewis, John L. "Copy Boy." *PM,* April 3, 1944, 14.
Lewis, John L. to Mr. F. W. McDonough, Editor. *Better Homes & Gardens,* April 27, 1948.
Lowenstein, Ralph. Comments about Rae Weimer, *Communigator,* Spring 1997.
Mackenzie, Ross. Quoted in Cunningham to Community Service Award. January 24, 1986.
Mackenzie, Ross. Service Above Self Award presentation, January 10, 1989, personal files of Rae Weimer.

MacPherson, Myra. *All Governments Lie! The Life and Times of Rebel Journalist I. F. Stone.* New York: A Lisa Drew Book/Scribner, 2006.

Margolick, David. "*PM*'s Impossible Dream." *Vanity Fair,* January 1999, 116–32.

Marston, Robert. Conferring of Honorary Degree, 1968, personal files of Rae Weimer.

Matthews, D. R. (Billy). Community Service Award, February 8, 1986, personal files of Rae Weimer.

Miami Herald. "Rae Weimer Obituary." November 16, 1996.

Milkman, Paul. *PM: A New Deal in Journalism 1940–1948.* Denver: Outskirts Press, 2016.

Moore, G. Paul. Community Service Award, February 6, 1986, personal files of Rae Weimer.

Moorehead, Jim. "Weimer Scholars." *Communigator*, Fall 1994, 18–19.

Morris, Bruce A. "It's the Magnetism Within." Unknown publication (n.d.).

Newbill, Mickey. Memo to Mr. Rae O. Weimer, June 13, 1957, personal files of Rae Weimer.

Niche. "2023 Best Colleges for Communications in America," https://www.niche.com/colleges/search/best-colleges-for-communications/ (accessed December 4, 2022).

O'Connell, Stephen C. "Dedication of Weimer Hall," October 24, 1981, personal files of Rae Weimer.

O'Connell, Stephen C. Community Service Award, February 12, 1986, personal files of Rae Weimer.

Ohio History Central. "Marion Steam Shovel Company." https://ohiohistorycentral.org/w/Marion_Steam_Shovel_Company (accessed February 5, 2022).

PM. "Prospectus to Sell 100,000 More *PM*s a Day." June 18, 1946.

Rowe, J. Ben. "Happy Birthday Rae O. Weimer." *Independent Farmer & Ranch,* November 3, 1983.

St. Petersburg Times. "Journalism Could Lead in New Educational Finance Methods," editorial, 1959.

Sedam, Lauren. "Wagon Reveals Part of History of Horse, Mule Markets." *Grand Island Independent,* January 6, 2016; updated September 24, 2019. https://theindependent.com/news/local/wagon-reveals-part-of-history-of-horse-mule-markets.

Sercombe, Ron. "Florida's Most Dynamic Dean." *Florida Newspaper News and Radio Digest* 49, no. 6 (July 1968).

Shonbrun, Margaret T. "On Rae Weimer, *PM,* and a Steamer Up the Hudson River to Bear Mountain." *Gainesville Sun,* July 19, 1983.

Simkin, John. "*PM* Newspaper." *Spartacus Educational,* September 1997; updated January 2020. https://spartacus-educational.com/PMnew.htm.

Smith, Richard K. *The Airships Akron & Macon: Flying Aircraft Carriers of the United States Navy.* Annapolis, Maryland: Naval Institute Press, 1965.

Stone, I. F. "The Meaning of the Associated Press Ruling." *PM,* June 20, 1945.

Stricker, Julie. "Busier Than Ever, Rae Weimer Recognized with Rotary Award." *Gainesville Sun,* January 11, 1989, 1D.

Sullivan, Frank. "Greetings, Friends!" *The New Yorker,* December 23, 1944, 25.

Sullivan, Frank, to Rae Weimer, July 20, 1945, personal files of Rae Weimer.

Taylor, A. "The Photography of Margaret Bourke-White." *The Atlantic,* August 28, 2019. https://www.theatlantic.com/photo/2019/08/photography-of-margaret-bourke-white/596980/.

Tunstall, Jim. "The Father of Florida Journalism." *Tampa Tribune,* August 17, 1994.

Wegman, Tad. "Dean Emeritus Weimer Misses Students at Journalism School." *Gainesville Sun,* May 2, 1977, front page.

Weimer, Rae O. Interview by Samuel Proctor, 1969, transcript of oral history interview, Department of History, University of Florida, November 4, 1974, personal files of Rae Weimer.

Weimer, Rae O. Personal notes from a speech given at Kearney State College, October 15, 1985. Quoted in Kirwan, "Rae Weimer: Pioneer of Journalism," May 1968, 14.

Weimer, Rae O. Talk at First Methodist Church Sunday School, February 22, 1987; Talk to a group of Engineers, April 20, 1987.

Weimer, Rae O. Personal interviews with Tom Kirwan in Gainesville, Florida, December 15 through February 1986.

Weimer, Rae O. Interview by Paul Milkman, 1994, for "*PM: A New Deal,*" personal files of Rae Weimer.

Wickware, Francis S. "Marshall Field III: He Tries to Atone for His Many Millions by Good Works and Profitless Journalism." *Life,* October 18, 1943, 102–118.

Wilkinson, Patricia. "Mr. Weimer Appreciated." *Gainesville Sun* (n.d.).

Index

Page numbers in *italics* refer to illustrations.

Ann Weimer Moxley, Rae's daughter, graduated from the University of Florida with a bachelor of arts with high honors in psychology, a master of science in psychology, and a PhD in clinical psychology. Almost twenty years later, she completed a postdoctorate in neuropsychology at the San Francisco VA Medical Center in California. Ann devoted her entire career to serving children and adults with disabilities, first at Monroe Developmental Center in Rochester, New York, then at the California School for the Deaf in Fremont, California, and also in her private neuropsychology practice. Ann and her second husband, James L. Solar, reside in Fairfield, California. Her goal in publishing this book is to tell her father's remarkable life story.